OECD ECONOMIC SURVEYS

1993-1994

TURKEY

ORGANISATION FOR ECONOMIC CO-OPERATION AND DEVELOPMENT

ORGANISATION FOR ECONOMIC CO-OPERATION AND DEVELOPMENT

Pursuant to Article 1 of the Convention signed in Paris on 14th December 1960, and which came into force on 30th September 1961, the Organisation for Economic Co-operation and Development (OECD) shall promote policies designed:

— to achieve the highest sustainable economic growth and employment and a rising standard of living in Member countries, while maintaining financial stability, and thus to contribute to the development of the world economy;
— to contribute to sound economic expansion in Member as well as non-member countries in the process of economic development; and
— to contribute to the expansion of world trade on a multilateral, non-discriminatory basis in accordance with international obligations.

The original Member countries of the OECD are Austria, Belgium, Canada, Denmark, France, Germany, Greece, Iceland, Ireland, Italy, Luxembourg, the Netherlands, Norway, Portugal, Spain, Sweden, Switzerland, Turkey, the United Kingdom and the United States. The following countries became Members subsequently through accession at the dates indicated hereafter: Japan (28th April 1964), Finland (28th January 1969), Australia (7th June 1971) and New Zealand (29th May 1973). The Commission of the European Communities takes part in the work of the OECD (Article 13 of the OECD Convention).

3 2280 00497 9639

Publié également en français.

Table of contents

Introduction   9

I. The economy in 1993 and near-term prospects   11

    Overview   11
    Accelerating expansion of demand and output   11
    ... but apparently weak response of the labour market   16
    Persistently high inflation   18
    A widening current external deficit   21
    Foreign debt   26
    The outlook to 1995   27

II. Economic policy   30

    Worsening fiscal deficits   30
    Monetary conditions determined by government financing
        requirements   45
    The interaction of currency substitution, seigniorage and inflation   54
    New initiatives in structural reform   59

III. Agricultural policy   63

    Introduction   63
    The socio-economics of Turkish agriculture   64
    The agronomy and geography of Turkish agriculture   70
    Agricultural support policies   74
    The implementation of agricultural policy   80
    Very recent developments   91

IV. Conclusions   93

Notes   99

References   108

Annex
  Calendar of main economic events   109

Statistical and structural annex   115

Box: State economic enterprises in the agri-food sector   81

Tables

Text

1.	Supply and use of resources	13
2.	Gross fixed investment by sector	16
3.	Main labour market indicators	17
4.	Prices	19
5.	Foreign trade	23
6.	Export performance	24
7.	Balance of payments	25
8.	External debt of Turkey	26
9.	Short-term projections	28
10.	Public sector borrowing requirement	31
11.	Central government budget	33
12.	Central government budget revenues	36
13.	Financing of the budget deficit	40
14.	Financial account of the non-financial State economic enterprises	42
15.	Assets and liabilities of the Central Bank	46
16.	Money and credit	48
17.	Interest rates	51
18.	Decomposition of the cost of non-preferential bank loans	52
19.	Seigniorage and inflation tax	57
20.	Value-added per employee in the agricultural and non-agricultural sectors	66
21.	Welfare indicators by province or region	66

22. Number and average size of farm holdings in Turkey, 1980 and 1990   68
23. Number of plots per farm holding, 1980 and 1990   69
24. Yields of major crops in Turkey   70
25. Regional agricultural output patterns   71
26. Producer subsidy equivalents   76
27. Consumer subsidy equivalents   79
28. Agricultural commodity price supports   84

Statistical and structural annex

A. National product   116
B. Supply and use of resources   118
C. Industrial production   119
D. Prices   120
E. Imports by commodities   121
F. Exports by commodities   122
G. Geographic distribution of foreign trade   123
H. Balance of payments   124
I. External debt of Turkey   125
J. Public sector borrowing   126
K. Money and banking   127
L. Central government budget   128
M. Central government budget revenues   129
N. Dollar exchange rate of the Turkish lira   130

Diagrams

Text

1. Macroeconomic performance   12
2. Contribution to real GNP growth   14
3. Decomposition of changes in the total domestic demand deflator   18
4. Trend of prices   20
5. Merchandise trade   22
6. Central government deficit and debt   34
7. Exchange rate developments   53

8.   Currency substitution   55

9.   Seigniorage and inflation   58

10. Actual and estimated changes in the GNP deflator   59

11. Share of agriculture in total employment and total output   64

12. Map of Turkey   67

13. Structure of agricultural support   78

14. Trends in agricultural trade   87

BASIC STATISTICS OF TURKEY

THE LAND

Area (thousand sq. km)	781	Major cities, 1990	
Agricultural area (thousand sq. km)	280	(thousand inhabitants):	
Forests (thousand sq. km)	202	Istanbul	7 427
		Ankara	3 236
		Izmir	2 680

THE PEOPLE

Population, 1992 (thousands)	58 090	Civilian labour force, 1992 (thousands)	20 319
Per sq. km, 1992	74	Civilian employment	18 738
Annual average rate of change		Agriculture, forestry, fishing	8 259
of population, 1992	2.3	Industry	3 298
		Construction	1 038
		Services	6 143

PRODUCTION

GNP, 1992 (TL billion)	779 462	Origin of GDP, 1992 (per cent):	
Per head (US$)	1 923	Agriculture, forestry, fishing	15.2
Gross fixed investment, 1992 (TL billion)	173 370	Industry	25.6
Per cent of GNP	22.2	Construction	6.4
Per head (US$)	47.5	Services	52.8

THE GOVERNMENT

Public consumption, 1992 (per cent of GNP)	17.5	Public debt, end-1992 (per cent of GNP)	61.7
Central government current revenue,		Domestic	26.0
1992 (per cent of GNP)	22.4	Foreign	35.7

FOREIGN TRADE

Commodity exports, 1992, fob		Commodity imports, 1992, cif	
(per cent of GNP)	13.1	(per cent of GNP)	20.4
Main exports (per cent of total exports):		Main imports (per cent of total imports):	
Agriculture	15.2	Machinery and equipment	25.3
Mining	1.8	Transport equipment	9.8
Industry	83.0	Base metals	11.7
		Oil	16.5

THE CURRENCY

Monetary unit: Turkish lira		Currency unit per US$,	
		average of daily figures:	
		1991	4 164.2
		1992	6 865.0
		1993	10 973.6

Note: An international comparison of certain basic statistics is given in an annex table.

This Survey is based on the Secretariat's study prepared for the annual review of Turkey by the Economic and Development Review Committee on 3rd February 1994.

•

After revisions in the light of discussions during the review, final approval of the Survey for publication was given by the Committee on 24 February 1994.

•

The previous Survey of Turkey was issued in April 1993.

Introduction

After a decade of impressive expansion and structural adjustment, the Turkish economy stagnated in 1991 as a result of the Gulf crisis and domestic political uncertainties. A new government, formed after early elections in October 1991, announced an economic programme aimed at lowering inflation through better macroeconomic discipline and returning to a path of higher output growth. In the event, the economy recovered in 1992 and output growth accelerated further in 1993, but the current external account swung into a deficit of 5 per cent of GNP. Inflation remained excessively high, and the economy's underlying financial imbalances continued to deteriorate steadily.

Contrary to government intentions, fiscal deficits widened in 1992 and 1993. With no assistance from fiscal policies there was hardly any scope for monetary policy to act to counter high inflation. As in the past, a large part of the burden on government budgets stemmed from State economic enterprises, but their restructuring and privatisation – high on the agenda of the new government – advanced very slowly. The momentum for structural reforms weakened, though progress was made in integrating important Extra-budgetary Funds into the central government budget as well as in further amending the Capital Market Law in 1992. Import tariffs were lowered and restructured to pave the way towards the customs union with the European Community 1995, which gave a new impetus to structural reform in certain areas.

Macroeconomic developments in 1993 and the outlook to 1995 are discussed in Part I of the present Survey. Part II presents an overview of budgetary and monetary developments in 1993 and policy objectives for 1994. Some discussion is also devoted to the issue of currency substitution and its relevance for monetary policy as well as to the interaction of monetary deficit financing and inflation. Then the latest structural policy initiatives are briefly sketched out. Part III reviews the main features of the Turkish agricultural sector and examines how efficient current agricultural policy is in meeting its distributional objectives as well as options that could alleviate the burden it poses on both the government budget and the economy more generally. The main findings of the report are summarised and conclusions for economic policy are drawn in Part IV.

I. The economy in 1993 and near-term prospects

Overview

Major indicators of macroeconomic performance bear witness to growing imbalances in the Turkish economy (Diagram 1), which call for corrective policy measures. Notwithstanding the weakness of economic activity in the OECD area and the consequent sluggish growth of export markets, Turkish real output growth accelerated to an average rate of nearly 7 per cent in 1993. Not surprisingly, the marked growth differential with the rest of the OECD threw the current external account into a sizeable deficit. A rather peculiar response to booming activity is the ongoing worsening of public sector financial positions. The only hesitant improvement in the labour market is also in some contrast to output buoyancy. Diverging inflation trends between Turkey and the average of the OECD are another striking feature of the current conjuncture, being not entirely the consequence of cyclical differences, but also of markedly different policy settings.

Accelerating expansion of demand and output

Growth of real output rebounded in 1992 and strengthened further in 1993, reaching a peak rate of nearly 11 per cent in the second quarter.[1] Production accelerated in industry and the services sectors (notably trade and transportation), while agricultural output remained rather flat (Table 1). The rate of manufacturing capacity utilisation improved by about 4 percentage points in 1993 on average, which could stimulate future business investment decisions.

The surge in real domestic demand in 1993 – estimated at 12½ per cent – was primarily driven by the unexpected boom in household consumption (Diagram 2). Household incomes were fuelled by real wage gains of around 7 per

Diagram 1. **MACROECONOMIC PERFORMANCE**

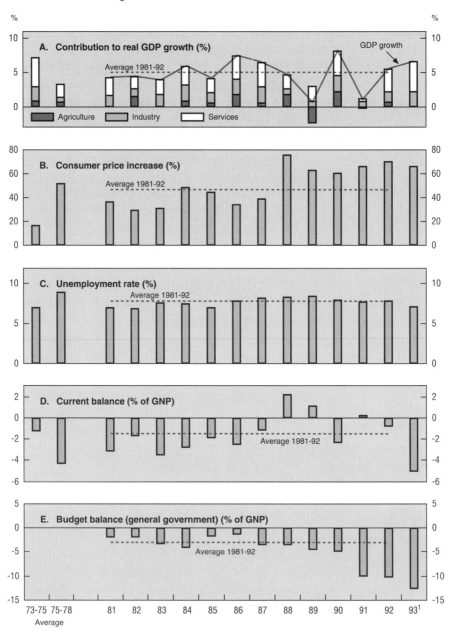

1. Estimates.
Sources: Data submitted by the State Planning Organisation, and OECD estimates.

Table 1. Supply and use of resources

	1992 Per cent of GNP in current prices	1990	1991	1992	1993 Programme	1993 Estimate	1994 Programme
		Percentage volume change					
Supply							
Agriculture	15.2	11.4	−1.2	3.7	3.0	0.1	3.0
Industry	25.6	9.0	2.7	5.8	6.0	8.1	5.4
Construction	6.4	−0.2	3.1	6.7	. .	. .	. .
Services	51.8	8.6	0.9	5.8	4.5	7.8	4.8
GDP	99.0	9.2	1.0	5.5	4.7	6.6	4.7
GNP (market prices)	100.0	9.2	0.5	5.9	5.0	6.8	4.5
Demand							
Private consumption	60.8	11.0	1.8	8.9	3.9	14.0	3.4
Public consumption	17.5	14.9	2.5	6.2	4.9	7.6	5.1
Private investment	12.1	18.7	−3.0	5.0	6.8	10.7	8.7
Public investment	10.1	6.2	4.5	1.8	−1.2	−2.5	2.4
Final domestic demand	100.5	11.8	1.4	7.4	3.9	11.4	4.2
Stockbuilding [1]	0.3	4.1	−3.9	0.5	1.2	1.1	−0.1
Total domestic demand	100.8	16.0	−2.2	7.9	5.0	12.4	4.0
Exports of goods and services	26.0	8.7	11.4	3.3	8.8	7.3	10.8
Imports of goods and services	25.2	32.0	−2.1	10.1	7.9	22.1	6.4
Foreign balance [1]	0.8	−6.5	2.8	−2.2	−0.2	−6.1	0.1
GNP price deflator		54.4	56.8	62.6	51.0	58.8	54.6
Memorandum items							
Domestic saving/GNP		23.5	22.6	21.6	19.7	19.4	20.4
Fixed investment/GNP		22.8	22.2	22.6	22.7	22.4	23.1

1. Contribution to GNP growth.
Source: State Planning Organisation and State Institute of Statistics.

cent in the private sector and close to 9 per cent for public sector workers (civil servants' real salaries, however, are reported to have grown on average by only some 2½ per cent in 1993). The wage hikes from 1989 to 1991, when real earnings in the unionised sector of the economy are estimated to have doubled, probably also have had a lagged stimulative effect on household spending behaviour in 1993. On the other hand, real incomes in the rural sector, accounting for roughly half of total employment, are likely to have stagnated, reflecting bad harvests for some farm products and a fall in agricultural support prices in real terms. With little evidence of any substantial boost to aggregate household

13

Diagram 2. **CONTRIBUTION TO REAL GNP GROWTH**

As a percentage change of GNP in previous year

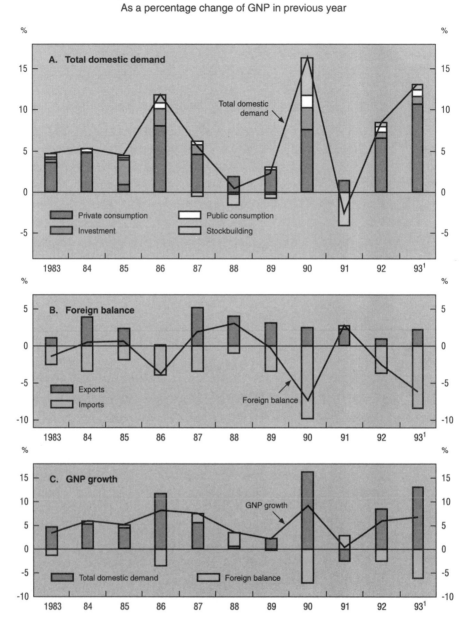

1. OECD estimates.
Source: State Institute of Statistics, *National Accounts.*

incomes from employment gains, the development of disposable incomes alone seems insufficient to explain the consumption boom. One important additional factor may have been the growing popularity of consumer credit, which until 1988 was virtually non-existent. Indeed, the legalisation of the securitisation of consumer credits in 1992 induced a dynamic expansion of this financing instrument. In combination with further liberalising of imports, the slump in most OECD economies and the real effective appreciation of the lira – all factors which tend to dampen import price increases – consumer goods imports have gained in attractiveness, which may further account for the surprising strength in private consumption. Largely because of concerns that strong consumption was leading to a rapid deterioration in the foreign balance, the government decided to restrict the use of asset-backed securities in 1994, limiting them to housing credits only.

Private investment appears to have been another driving force of accelerating economic activity, notwithstanding the very high real lending rates (see below) on the one hand and highly attractive yields on government instruments on the other; obviously, private investors resorted massively to foreign borrowing. Private investment in the housing, transport and communications and agriculture sectors, covering more than two-thirds of the total, posted the most dynamic expansion (Table 2). Private manufacturing investment, less than one-third of total private investment, grew by 7½ per cent in volume, thereby lagging behind domestic demand. Sound profitability of enterprises in spite of the surge in labour costs since 1988 and reported efforts to substitute capital for labour seem to have remained supportive of business investment. Tentative estimates of labour productivity indeed suggest strong improvements in recent years; nearly all of the output growth in 1993 seems to be attributable to productivity gains.

In stark contrast to the private sector, real public investment in manufacturing fell by more than 40 per cent, so that total investment volumes in manufacturing broadly stagnated. This does not augur well in view of preparations for the customs union with the European Community envisaged for 1995 (see below), which certainly will raise the intensity of competition in many exposed sectors of the economy, including those dominated by public sector manufacturing enterprises. The fall in total public investment is clearly a reflection of the growing financial constraints of the public sector, while the acceleration of real government consumption largely mirrors spending for defence and security.

Table 2. **Gross fixed investment by sector**

	1991 Share in current prices	1989	1990	1991	1992	1993 Estimate	1994 Programme
		Percentage changes, volume					
Private sector							
Agriculture	4.2	−27.2	46.0	−11.6	0.8	19.9	6.3
Mining	1.3	2.2	5.5	0.5	−9.8	−10.3	6.4
Manufacturing	27.6	−4.3	63.7	−1.4	0.2	7.5	5.6
Energy[1]	1.9	29.1	−13.4	46.0	−46.9	−2.6	283.4
Transport and communication	13.0	−0.7	55.0	3.7	42.6	27.2	9.8
Tourism	6.0	37.7	9.9	−5.0	−11.9	−45.7	1.7
Housing	40.5	6.3	−8.0	−8.7	0.3	12.7	5.0
Education	0.7	27.0	26.1	15.9	7.0	3.7	3.6
Health	1.3	51.8	57.6	45.6	7.1	−8.6	11.5
Other services	3.4	4.7	10.9	0.6	5.2	10.2	5.0
Total	100.0 (54.2)	3.2	18.7	−3.0	5.0	10.7	8.7
Public sector							
Agriculture	11.3	6.3	−5.3	18.6	−20.9	14.9	−3.1
Mining	3.5	−33.1	12.6	2.3	−6.6	−20.2	−7.8
Manufacturing	5.1	−27.6	5.3	20.1	8.1	−43.5	−4.7
Energy[1]	17.0	4.3	−21.9	−20.0	−13.9	−6.8	11.0
Transport and communication	37.1	−3.7	19.7	12.4	−1.6	−5.1	−9.5
Tourism	1.5	−33.5	12.0	41.2	3.8	5.2	15.8
Housing	2.1	−2.0	118.4	−45.2	17.1	−16.4	0.9
Education	6.4	3.0	19.5	0.9	26.9	14.8	10.2
Health	2.5	17.2	37.0	−4.3	27.6	10.1	7.5
Other services	13.4	−24.6	21.3	27.3	25.8	4.4	16.7
Total	100.0 (45.8)	−5.8	6.1	4.5	1.8	−2.5	2.4
Total gross fixed investment	(100.0)	−1.1	13.0	0.2	3.6	4.9	6.1

1. Electricity, gas and water.
Source: Data provided by the State Planning Organisation.

... but apparently weak response of the labour market

Labour market statistics remain very deficient[2] and sometimes contradictory. In spite of strong economic growth, available data suggest a rise in total employment of only 1 per cent in 1992, which results from an employment increase in industry and in the services sector by 7½ and 8 per cent, respectively, combined with a fall of employment in agriculture by about 6 per cent (Table 3). The

Table 3. **Main labour market indicators**[1]

	Thousand				Percentage change over previous year			
	1990 October	1991 October	1992 October	1993 April	1990	1991	1992	1993/92 April
Population, age 15 and over	34 073	34 119	36 544		2.1	1.4	2.5	
Participation ratio (per cent)	59	58	56					
Civilian labour force	20 163	19 789	20 319	20 081	1.2	0.3	1.1	1.0
Civilian employment	18 681	18 171	18 738	18 633	2.0	0.3	1.0	0.9
By sector (per cent of total)								
Agriculture	46.1	48.0	43.9	47.0	1.1	2.6	−6.3	8.4
Mining and energy	1.2	1.3	1.4	1.1	9.0	−13.5	9.6	25.9
Manufacturing	14.5	13.7	16.2	13.6	1.8	3.6	7.2	−3.3
Construction	4.8	5.2	5.0	6.3	−7.3	5.2	9.4	24.2
Transport	4.6	4.2	4.7	4.4	3.6	−3.3	6.8	−3.9
Trade[2]	11.6	11.8	12.0	12.0	6.5	2.2	9.4	−1.3
Other services	17.2	16.9	15.6	15.6	7.8	−2.6	5.1	−17.5
Unemployed	1 482	1 618	1 581	1 448				
Unemployment rate (per cent)								
Total	7.3	8.2	7.8	7.2				
Urban	10.7	12.0	11.7	10.9				
Rural	4.8	5.2	4.7	4.1				
Memorandum item								
Unemployment rate plus under-employment	14.3	14.7	15.1	13.8				

1. In 1988, the State Institute of Statistics started a bi-annual Household Labour Force Survey. The labour market statistics for the period of 1978-87 were revised on the basis of the 1988 Survey, sectoral value-added and productivity estimates. From 1988 onwards, Survey results have been used. Annual percentage changes are based on the averages of April and October Surveys.
2. From 1988 onwards, trade includes tourism services too.
Source: State Institute of Statistics, *Household Labour Force Surveys*, and data provided by the State Planning Organisation.

April 1993 Household Labour Force Survey (HLFS) suggests a further twelve-monthly growth of total employment by 1 per cent, but this time decreases were recorded for both industry[3] and services while agricultural employment is estimated to have risen rapidly. The marked contrast of the reported employment changes to sectoral developments in value-added casts serious doubts about the reliability of the HLFS and calls for an inquiry.

The rate of unemployment is measured to have fallen by only 1/2 percentage point during 1992; it seems to have decreased further, by 3/4 percentage point to 71/4 per cent, during the 12 months to April 1993. At 11 per cent, urban unemployment remained much higher than rural unemployment (4 per cent in

April 1993). A particularly pressing problem is the 30 per cent unemployment rate of the educated young (those aged 15 to 24 years with upper secondary schooling or university degree). The labour force participation rate is reported to have continued its trend decline, which is related to increasing educational attainment and the effects of internal migration on female labour participation.

Persistently high inflation

Since 1988, when the average annual rate of consumer price inflation roughly doubled to about 74 per cent, annual inflation has broadly stayed in the 60 to 70 per cent range. The fact that – for example – annual inflation averaged 63 and 66 per cent in 1989 and 1991, respectively, when activity more or less stagnated, reveals its relative lack of sensitivity to the economy's cyclical position. With the wage share in national income falling again to some 35 per cent in 1992, after the wage hikes of 1989 to 1991, the impact of changes in labour cost on inflation is relatively limited (Diagram 3). This is consistent with earlier

Diagram 3. **DECOMPOSITION OF CHANGES IN THE TOTAL DOMESTIC DEMAND DEFLATOR**

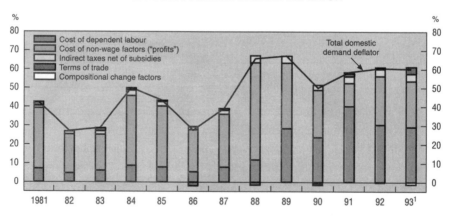

Note: This diagram gives an "accounting" breakdown of the rise in the total domestic demand deflator. The decomposition does not seek to explain inflation in causal terms, since all items in the breakdown are interdependent.
1. Provisional estimates.
Source: OECD.

Table 4. **Prices**[1]

Percentage change over previous year, annual and quarterly averages

(Base year 1987 = 100)

| | Wholesale prices | | | | | | | Consumer prices | |
| | General index | | | | | | | | |
	Total	Public	Private	Agriculture	Mining	Manufacturing	Energy	General	Food
Weights	(100.0)	(27.74)	(72.26)	(23.03)	(2.54)	(69.80)	(4.62)	(100.0)	(32.1)
1988	70.5	70.3	70.5	44.1	64.1	81.5	40.9	73.7	83.2
1989	64.0	64.2	63.9	71.7	65.0	61.6	69.2	63.2	69.3
1990	52.3	56.7	50.6	70.6	48.7	46.9	56.5	60.3	64.3
1991	55.3	61.3	53.0	50.8	63.2	55.3	75.1	66.0	67.1
Q1	49.7	59.4	46.0	42.8	56.3	50.9	64.5	62.6	63.1
Q2	56.5	65.5	53.0	48.4	74.5	58.2	61.7	63.2	59.3
Q3	57.5	69.2	52.8	44.7	70.1	59.5	82.3	68.7	69.0
Q4	56.7	53.0	58.2	65.6	54.8	52.6	88.6	68.1	74.8
1992	62.1	65.2	60.8	62.7	61.6	59.7	97.7	70.1	71.3
Q1	68.7	66.5	69.5	91.1	62.9	59.0	111.6	78.4	90.2
Q2	60.1	61.8	51.3	67.4	56.5	55.1	103.6	69.8	72.0
Q3	58.2	62.9	56.2	47.3	65.0	58.9	90.7	66.4	63.7
Q4	62.4	69.0	59.7	50.4	57.4	64.6	90.3	67.9	64.3
1993	58.4	54.5	60.1	62.2	56.7	56.6	67.8	66.1	63.5
Q1	52.9	52.2	53.2	37.2	51.9	58.1	64.3	58.6	48.9
Q2	57.3	54.9	58.3	52.2	60.6	58.4	66.2	63.6	60.7
Q3	62.8	56.1	65.8	86.2	53.0	56.6	66.8	70.8	72.9
Q4	66.3	59.3	69.3	85.8	66.5	54.1	77.8	69.3	69.5
Dec. 93/92	60.3	55.2	62.5	75.6	63.9	54.6	75.1	71.7	72.7
Jan. 94/93	60.6	57.9	61.8	70.7	65.5	56.6	70.1	69.6	69.8
Feb. 94/93	68.0	64.0	69.4	69.4	68.0	67.6	69.3	73.0	74.7

1. In January 1990, the State Institute of Statistics introduced new weights for both wholesale and consumer price indices, and changed the base year of the consumer price index from 1978-79 to 1987. In January 1991, the base year for the wholesale index was changed from 1981 to 1987.

Source: State Institute of Statistics, *Price Indices Monthly Bulletin*.

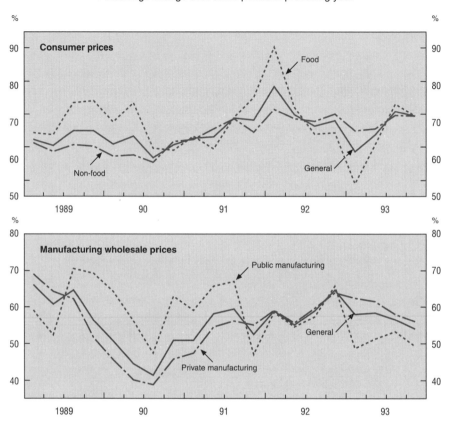

Diagram 4. **TREND OF PRICES**

Percentage change over same period of preceding year

Source: State Institute of Statistics, *Price Indices Monthly Bulletin.*

findings that the high and now firmly ingrained inflationary forces in the Turkish economy are primarily a reflection of public-sector deficits and their monetisation, a relationship which is re-examined further below.

Short-term aggregate price fluctuations often go hand in hand with changes in food prices in response to harvests and hence to the weather, as well as changes in administered prices, world energy- or raw-material prices, indirect tax rates and the exchange rate. In the first half of 1993, a slowdown in the pace of depreciation of the lira, increased supply of moderately priced foreign goods and the government's tighter control of price setting of some of the State economic enterprises all helped to bring inflation rates down from their high levels of the end of 1992[4] (Table 4). A bad harvest of fruit and vegetables and a shortage of meat induced an acceleration of inflation in the second half of 1993, in spite of weakening prices of imported energy.[5] Wholesale price inflation in manufactures displayed some further slowdown in the autumn of 1993 (Diagram 4). However, a rise in value-added tax rates as from November 1993 pushed consumer price inflation up further by the end of the year. Altogether, the annual CPI inflation averaged 66 per cent in 1993, after 70 per cent in 1992.

A widening current external deficit

Provisional estimates suggest a current account deficit of $5 billion in 1993, about 5 per cent of GNP, the highest deficit/GNP ratio since 1980, when it amounted to 5.8 per cent. The Turkish current external position already deteriorated in 1990 when the trade deficit more than doubled and the current account swung from a surplus of 1.2 per cent of GNP in 1989 into a deficit of 2.4 per cent. During the economic stagnation of 1991, lower imports and higher official grants led to a small current external surplus. But in 1992, import demand recovered and notwithstanding the revived export drive, the current account again turned into a deficit of 0.8 per cent of GNP.

The already large trade deficit widened further (Diagram 5), from 7 per cent of GNP in 1992 to over 11 per cent in 1993. Consequent upon vigorous expansion of domestic demand, merchandise import volume growth accelerated from 10.5 per cent in 1992 to 28 per cent in 1993. High household consumption boosted the import of consumer goods (notably automobiles), which reached a share of almost 14 per cent of total imports. But imports of investment goods and semi-finished products were also booming, increasing by about 30 per cent in dollar value (Table 5). Import demand is likely to have been stimulated by favourable relative import prices, which reflected ongoing disinflation in the OECD area, the strength of the Turkish lira in real effective terms in 1993 as well as cuts in customs tariffs; easier access to supplier credits also seems to have facilitated imports.

21

Diagram 5. **MERCHANDISE TRADE**
$ million, seasonally adjusted

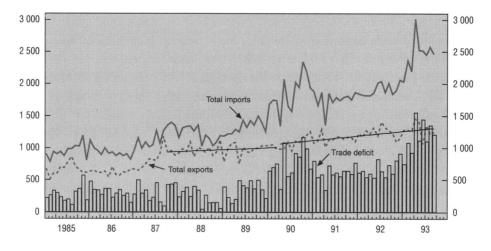

Source: OECD, *Monthly Statistics of Foreign Trade.*

Growth of merchandise export volumes appears to have slowed from 8.0 per cent in 1992 to close to 4 per cent in 1993. However, this conceals a relatively good export performance in the context of shrinking export markets (Table 6). Export performance could have been even better, had it not been for deteriorating price competitiveness due to real exchange-rate appreciation. The main contribution to total goods export growth came from manufactures, in particular textiles and clothing, followed by iron and steel products, while agricultural exports virtually stagnated.

The surplus in the services account is estimated to have increased by about $1 billion. Apart from higher tourism revenues and workers' remittances this was largely due to a marked upswing in "other service incomes" (Table 7). Much of the buoyancy of the latter item stems from an increase in interest earnings and other investment income, like contractors' fees, as well as strong transport revenues as a result of the trade surge. Revenues from tourism had been depressed in the period just after the Gulf crisis, but began picking up at the beginning of 1992. In 1992, tourist arrivals increased by 28 per cent to 7.5 million persons.

Table 5.   **Foreign trade**[1]

	1992 $ million	1990	1991	1992	1992				1993		
					Q1	Q2	Q3	Q4	Q1	Q2	Q3
					Percentage change over previous year						
Exports (fob)											
Agriculture	2 304	10.4	14.3	-17.9	-2.7	23.2	-34.5	-31.3	9.3	-14.4	32.2
Mining and quarrying	264	-19.7	-13.8	-7.7	27.8	-4.5	-14.1	-27.2	-33.3	-23.8	-1.4
Manufacturing	12 247	13.1	3.3	15.3	6.4	12.8	28.0	14.7	3.1	9.1	-6.0
Total	14 715	11.5	4.9	8.3	5.1	13.7	15.4	1.6	3.5	5.3	-3.8
Average value		9.1	-1.7	0.3							
Volume		3.2	6.7	8.0							
Imports (cif)											
Consumption goods	2 954	117.6	-3.7	0.9	-9.3	-7.8	9.4	9.0	20.6	71.9	34.7
Investment goods	6 825	50.5	4.6	13.5	14.9	37.0	2.2	5.9	12.7	40.9	52.7
Raw materials	13 092	27.8	-10.4	8.1	-3.4	11.1	17.3	7.6	22.9	36.9	14.1
of which: Oil	2 632	42.3	-29.3	7.2	-14.5	20.0	22.3	1.9	22.3	-7.4	-24.0
Total	22 871	41.2	-5.7	8.7	0.5	15.6	11.7	7.3	19.5	42.0	27.3
Average value		2.8	-3.9	-1.6							
Volume		37.4	-1.9	10.5							

1. Excluding transit trade and imports of non-monetary gold.
Source: State Planning Organisation, *Monthly Indicators.*

23

Table 6. **Export performance**

Change in per cent

	1990	1991	1992	1993 Estimates
Volumes				
Merchandise exports	2.2	6.7	8.0	3.8
Export markets	6.3	6.2	3.0	−2.6
Relative export performance[1]	−3.9	0.5	4.9	6.6
Prices (in TL)				
Export prices	62.8	57.2	65.5	61.8
Unit labour cost	88.5	116.8	66.2	64.5
Profit margins[2]	−13.6	−27.5	−0.4	−1.6

1. Differential between export growth and export market growth.
2. Differential between export price and unit labour cost growth.
Source: State Planning Organisation and OECD.

Tourism revenues rose even faster, by 37 per cent, reflecting the growing share of tourists from OECD countries with relatively high propensity to spend. However, recent data indicate a decline in the number of tourist arrivals and thereby a considerable slowdown in tourism revenue growth during 1993. Official transfers continued to trend downward as official grants compensating for losses from the Gulf War petered out.

Turkey had no apparent problem in raising some $10 billion needed altogether in 1993 to finance the current account deficit and to repay foreign debt. In fact, total capital inflows were strong enough to push up foreign exchange reserves by some $1½ billion. However, the increase in foreign direct investment remained rather modest: the long-awaited break-through in foreign direct investment in Turkey has yet to come. On the other hand, foreign portfolio investment considerably exceeded government projections. The Treasury was the most important borrower, raising $3.4 billion in international capital markets (mainly 5 to 10 years maturity). Other credits were mostly project credits ($3 billion) from multinational and bilateral sources including suppliers, either contracted in 1993 or unused portions of earlier credit arrangements. In addition, some $700 million were borrowed from commercial banks and another $800 million expected through the Dresdner Bank scheme.[6] Turkey's repayments on foreign debt in

Table 7. **Balance of payments**

$ million

	1989	1990	1991	1992	1993 November	1993 Estimate [1]	1994 Programme
Current account							
Exports (fob) [2]	11 780	13 026	13 667	14 891	13 654	15 400	17 540
Imports (fob) [2]	−15 999	−22 581	−21 007	−23 082	−26 523	−28 760	−30 690
Trade balance	−4 219	−9 555	−7 340	−8 191	−12 869	−13 360	−13 240
Services and income, credit	7 098	8 933	9 315	10 451	10 928	12 300	13 500
Tourism	2 557	3 225	2 654	3 639	3 802	3 900	4 700
Investment income	1 266	1 658	1 635	1 999	2 046	..	..
Other	3 275	4 050	5 026	4 813	5 080	7 300	7 500
Services and income, debit	−5 476	−6 496	−6 816	−7 262	−7 076	−7 950	−8 650
Tourism	−565	−520	−592	−776	−863	−950	−1 000
Interest payments	−2 907	−3 264	−3 430	−3 217	−3 153	−3 600	−4 000
Other	−2 004	−2 712	−2 794	−3 269	−3 051	−3 400	−3 650
Private transfers, net	3 135	3 349	2 854	3 147	2 791	3 280	3 300
Official transfers, net	423	1 144	2 245	912	676	720	630
Invisibles balance	5 180	6 930	7 598	7 248	7 328	8 350	8 780
Current balance	961	−2 625	258	−943	−5 541	−5 010	−4 460
Capital account							
Direct investment	663	700	783	779	529	875	1 100
Portfolio investment	1 586	547	648	2 411	3 786	4 000	1 835
Credit utilisation	2 620	3 679	3 784	3 523	4 424	4 200	4 680
Dresdner Bank scheme, net	518	49	−497	410	830	800	700
Debt repayments	−4 023	−3 938	−4 095	−4 871	−4 061	−4 700	−4 850
Capital balance	1 364	1 037	623	2 252	5 508	5 175	3 465
Basic balance	2 325	−1 588	895	1 309	−33	165	−995
Short-term capital	−584	3 000	−3 020	1 396	3 771	2 150	1 995
Assets	371	−409	−2 563	−2 458	−674	−1 100	300
Credits extended	390	156	−811	24	117	500	500
Bank reserves	−19	−565	−1 752	−2 482	−791	−1 600	−200
Liabilities	−955	3 409	−457	3 834	4 445	3 250	1 695
Credits received	−1 227	2 520	590	4 090	4 031	3 000	1 500
Deposits	272	889	−1 047	−258	414	250	195
Errors and omissions	971	−468	940	−1 221	−2 489	−815	0
Counterpart items	50	364	170	0	0	0	0
Overall balance	2 762	1 308	−1 029	1 484	1 249	1 500	1 000
Change in official reserves	−2 762	−1 308	1 029	−1 484	−1 249	−1 500	−1 000
Official reserves	−2 510	−1 255	1 029	−1 484	−1 249	−1 500	−1 000
IMF	−252	−53	0	0	0	0	0

1. Estimate made in October 1993.
2. Including transit trade.
Source: Central Bank of Turkey, *Quarterly Bulletin* and State Planning Organisation.

dollar terms are estimated to have remained slightly below those in 1992, owing largely to the depreciation of other currencies against the dollar.

Foreign debt

Consequent upon the widening current external deficit, total foreign disbursed debt rose by about $5 billion during 1993 to over $60 billion at year-end.

Table 8. **External debt of Turkey**

Disbursed debt – end of period

$ million

	1987	1988	1989	1990	1991	1992	1993 June[1]
Medium- and long-term debt	32 605	34 305	36 006	39 535	41 372	42 932	44 896
Multilateral creditors	9 802	9 192	8 740	9 564	10 069	9 160	9 043
Bilateral creditors	11 680	11 382	11 431	12 984	14 587	15 035	15 346
Commercial banks	6 391	8 891	10 269	10 720	10 992	12 956	14 506
Private lenders	4 732	4 840	5 566	6 267	5 724	5 781	6 001
Short-term debt	7 623	6 417	5 745	9 500	9 117	12 660	14 485
Credits	5 004	3 984	2 950	5 524	6 134	10 065	11 878
Deposits	2 619	2 433	2 795	3 976	2 983	2 595	2 607
Total debt	40 228	40 722	41 751	49 035	50 489	55 592	59 381
Memorandum items (per cent)							
Total debt/GNP	58.8	57.5	52.0	44.5	46.5	49.1	..
Medium- and long-term debt/GNP	47.6	48.5	44.8	35.9	38.1	38.0	..
Short-term debt/GNP	11.1	9.1	7.1	8.6	8.4	11.2	..
Short-term debt/total debt	18.9	15.8	13.8	19.4	18.1	22.8	24.4
Total debt/export of goods and services	237.6	202.3	185.8	185.1	179.6	189.1	..
Medium- and long-term debt by borrower as per cent of total debt							
General government	51.0	54.6	55.2	52.2	54.2	51.2	50.8
SEE's	9.2	9.8	10.5	9.8	10.3	9.2	8.4
Central Bank	17.6	16.1	16.7	14.9	12.9	11.1	10.7
Private sector	3.3	3.7	3.8	3.7	4.5	5.7	5.7
Debt service/GNP	8.1	10.1	8.9	6.6	6.9	7.2	..
Debt service/exports of goods and services	32.6	35.6	31.9	27.4	26.8	27.5	..
Average maturity (year)	16.0	15.3	15.0	15.1	14.6	14.0	13.4
Average spread over LIBOR	1.0	0.9	1.2	0.9	1.0	1.6	1.5

1. Provisional.
Source: Data provided by the Under-Secretariat of the Treasury and Foreign Trade, and Central Bank of Turkey.

The debt/GNP ratio, which had declined from a peak of 59 per cent in 1987 to 45 per cent in 1990, rose again thereafter, to an estimated 55 per cent at the end of 1993. Another indicator for a country's solvency, the debt/export ratio, also edged up in 1992 and 1993, after a long period of substantial decline (Table 8).

The level of short-term debt almost tripled between 1989 and 1993; during this period its share in total debt rose from some 14 to around 25 per cent. The shortening of debt maturity reflects in part the increasing weight in foreign debt of trade credits and foreign currency deposits. But the structure of general government debt, still dominated by medium and long-term borrowing, is also gradually shifting to shorter maturities, mirroring the replacement of concessional credits by heavier borrowing from commercial sources. The debt-service/GNP ratio, which had decreased from 10.1 per cent in 1988 to 6.9 per cent in 1991, increased to 7.2 per cent in 1992. However, the ratio of debt service to exports of goods and services fell from 35.6 per cent in 1988 to 27.5 per cent in 1992, a trend which continued in 1993.

The outlook to 1995

The projections by the OECD Secretariat presented below assume that after the local elections in March 1994, the government will take more determined steps to discipline public finances. These would include some restraint on spending of State economic enterprises and further measures to raise government revenues, for which there is a large potential, given that the share of total tax revenues in GNP, currently about 32 per cent (including social security contributions), is among the lowest in the OECD area. However, the amendments to the tax laws of December 1993 will show their full revenue effect only as from 1995. On the other hand, this year and thereafter, privatisation revenues may increase faster than in the past. On this basis, the public-sector borrowing requirement may be contained, which would ease the upward pressure on interest rates and thereby offer some relief for future budgets. It is also assumed that from February 1994 on, the lira exchange rate depreciates in line with the inflation differential between Turkey and the (trade-weighted) average of its partner countries.

GNP growth is projected to return to more sustainable rates of about 4 per cent in 1994 and around 5 per cent in 1995 (Table 9). With the effect on incomes of earlier wage hikes subsiding, current and future wage developments projected

Table 9. **Short-term projections**

Percentage changes, volume (1982 prices)

	1991 Current prices billion TL	Per cent of GDP	1993 Estimate	1994	1995
				Projections[3]	
Private consumption	279 430	61.7	14.0	3.8	4.1
Government consumption	72 175	15.9	7.6	5.0	3.8
Private investment	55 578	12.2	10.7	6.5	7.8
Public investment	46 815	10.4	-2.5	1.0	1.0
Final domestic demand	453 998	100.2	11.8	4.0	4.3
Change in stockbuilding[1]	-1 863	-0.4	0.8	-0.3	-0.0
Total domestic demand	452 135	99.8	12.4	3.7	4.2
Exports of goods and services	117 198	25.9	7.3	7.8	10.4
Imports of goods and services	116 126	25.6	22.4	5.8	6.5
Change in foreign balance[1]	1 072	0.2	-6.2	-0.0	0.6
GNP at market prices	453 207	100.0	7.0	4.1	5.2
GNP implicit price deflator	-		58.8	75.0	70.0
Memorandum items					
Consumer prices	-		66.0	78.0	73.0
Unemployment rate	-		7.2	8.0	9.0
Current balance ($ million)	-		-5.9	-5.0	-4.5
Current balance[2]			-5.2	-5.1	-3.7

1. As a percentage of GNP in the previous period.
2. As a percentage of GNP.
3. Projections are based on the information available at the beginning of February 1994.
Source: OECD.

to display more moderation and real incomes suffering from inflationary erosion, growth of household consumption is likely to decelerate sharply from its exceptional pace of 1993. Private investment should also slow down, hit hard by the surge in interest rates in the wake of the foreign exchange market crisis in January 1994. With the situation gradually normalising and export demand picking up, private investment should gain strength in 1995, reinforced by stronger foreign direct investment. Preparations of industry for the customs union with the European Community and for the expected concomitant intensification of international competition are also likely to support business investment this year and next. The expected flat profile of public investment volumes is a reflection of the critical situation of government finances. The projected recovery in foreign markets, together with the recent sharp depreciation of the Turkish lira should give a boost to merchandise exports. On the other hand, tourism revenues are likely to remain subdued. Import growth is expected to slow down in line with domestic demand and consequent upon exchange rate-induced import price increases. Altogether, the current external account will remain in deficit, perhaps of the order of 5 per cent of GNP in 1994 and 3¾ per cent in 1995.

Given the recent fall in the lira exchange rate, increased value-added tax rates and higher public-sector deficits, inflation is projected to rise substantially in 1994 before slowing down somewhat in 1995, though remaining exceptionally high by OECD standards. Stabilisation should be supported by the likely reduction of domestic demand pressure and wage moderation in response to rising labour market slack. With continued rapid growth of the labour force exceeding the projected employment increase, the unemployment rate may rise to 9 per cent by 1995.

The projections hinge crucially upon the actual conduct of fiscal policy. Failure to bring the deterioration in the public-sector financial positions to a halt would almost inevitably lead to inflation even higher than projected and risk severely impairing the government's credibility and financial market stability. This in turn would impart further upward pressure on interest rates, which would boost government debt service payments. The consequent further worsening of public sector finances would then add to inflation pressures. Moreover, higher interest rates could weaken Turkey's international competitiveness through crowding out of private investment by the public sector. External payments positions could then deteriorate further. In short, it is clear that the situation will become increasingly unsustainable without determined fiscal consolidation efforts.

II. Economic policy

The long awaited bold move towards macro-economic equilibrium did not occur in 1993. Public sector financial deficits continued to rise in relation to GNP and so did the share of interest payments in total expenditure. This barely left any scope for monetary policy to make inroads into high inflation without risking serious damage to the economy. Important reform projects, long on the political agenda, have either stalled or progressed much less than envisaged a year ago, although the prospective formation of a customs union with the European Community by 1995 has given some renewed impetus to structural reform efforts.

Worsening fiscal deficits

Public sector borrowing requirements

The extent of failure to bring the government's house in order is clearly shown in the public sector borrowing requirement (PSBR): instead of coming down from about 15 per cent of GNP in 1992 to the 9 per cent programmed for 1993, the PSBR/GNP ratio even rose further to an estimated 16.3 per cent, the highest ever recorded. The lion's share of this slippage was due to the consolidated central government deficit (Table 10). It turned out to be more than double the target – an estimated 9.2 per cent of GNP in 1993[7] as compared with the programmed 4.3 per cent – a particularly disappointing outcome in view of stronger economic activity and higher inflation than earlier envisaged. Most of the gap between the actual and planned central government deficit is attributable to higher expenditures. The SEEs' borrowing need shrank by 1 per cent of GNP, but this was at the expense of a worsening of the central government's finances.[8] Even so, the reduction in borrowing by the SEEs fell short of the target.

Table 10. **Public sector borrowing requirement**

	1989	1990	1991	1992	1993 Programme	1993 Estimate[1]	1994 Programme
Public sector deficit (PSBR)							
(TL trillion)	12.3	29.3	65.6	116.5	110.2	215.9	303.7
General government	7.9	14.3	45.7	79.5	77.9	167.9	243.5
State economic enterprises (SEEs)	4.4	15.0	19.9	37.0	32.3	48.0	60.2
PSBR/GNP							
(per cent)	7.2	10.2	14.5	14.9	9.0	16.3	14.2
General government	4.5	4.9	10.1	10.2	6.4	12.7	11.4
Central government	4.5	4.2	7.4	6.1	4.3	9.2	9.0
Local administrations	0.3	0	0.7	1.1	0.3	0.9	0.2
Social security institutions	−0.5	−0.4	0.2	0.3	0.1	1.2	1.3
Extra-budgetary funds (EBFs)[2]	0.3	1.1	1.8	2.8	1.7	1.4	0.9
SEEs[3]	2.6	5.3	4.4	4.7	2.6	3.6	2.8
Financing PSBR (per cent of total)							
Central Bank	3.7	1.5	16.5	20.1	24.5	23.2	23.6
Foreign borrowing, net	15.5	12.7	3.3	14.0	6.8	5.4	4.5
Domestic borrowing, net	80.8	85.8	80.2	65.9	68.7	71.4	71.9
Memorandum items							
Public debt/GNP							
General government	53.7	43.5	43.2	48.7	..	54.8	..
Domestic	25.3	20.2	20.0	23.4	..	29.3	..
Foreign	28.4	23.3	23.2	25.3	..	25.5	..
SEEs' foreign debt	5.1	4.4	4.5	4.5	..	4.3	..
Central Bank foreign debt	9.7	7.4	6.5	5.9	..	5.7	..
General government primary deficit/GNP	−0.9	−0.1	−4.4	−3.7	−0.3	−0.4	+
PSBR/GNP (excluding grants)	7.2	10.8	16.2	15.4	9.1	16.5	14.2

1. Estimate made in October 1993, when the 1994 Budget was prepared.
2. Consolidated financial accounts of 11 EBFs, including 8 large EBFs whose revenues and expenditures have been integrated in the Central Government budget since 1993. SEEs in the process of privatisation which have been transferred to the Public Participation Administration are included in EBFs.
3. Including non-financial SEEs.
Source: Data provided by the State Planning Organisation, and OECD estimates.

The estimated cut in the Extra-budgetary Funds' (EBF) deficit from 2.8 per cent of GNP in 1992 to 1.4 per cent in 1993, is a greater improvement than envisaged in the initial budget. This resulted from higher revenues as well as expenditure control imposed by the integration of a large number of EBFs into the central government budget.[9] Revenues for EBFs in 1993 may, however, be overestimated as the expected strong increase in privatisation proceeds, half of which may in principle be kept with the Public Participation Fund, is unlikely to be realised (see below). The social security system contributed to the rise in overall PSBR as companies (including SEEs) continued the practice of deferring the transfer of withheld contributions to the social security system.[10] Another source of the social security system's deficit is the early retirement scheme of the public sector, which has been introduced in 1992.

In 1994, the PSBR is planned to decline to 14 per cent of GNP, the fiscal adjustment of about 2 per cent of GNP to be equally shared between the general government and the SEEs. In view of the rigidity of almost all expenditure items, most of it is expected to be brought about by stronger revenues.

The central government account in 1993

Expenditures

Central government expenditures are estimated to have grown by some 118 per cent in 1993, thereby grossly exceeding their projected growth rate of about 80 per cent (Table 11).[11] As in previous years, most of the expenditure overrun originated in debt interest payments and the government wage bill – the two items together accounting for about 60 per cent of the spending overrun.

Interest payments exhibited the most dynamic expansion, rising by 191 per cent in 1993 in stark contrast to the programme target of 81 per cent. Interest payments on domestic debt more than tripled, reflecting both higher-than-expected interest rates and the growing domestic debt stock (Diagram 6). The increase here is, however, exaggerated somewhat by the fact that TL 6.4 trillion of interest payments already paid in 1992 were recorded in the 1993 budget, following the government accounting procedures. Another factor which boosted interest payments in 1993 was the shortening of the maturity of the debt stock, which ran diametrically counter to the planned borrowing strategy of the government.[12] Given the strong growth of external borrowing, the substantial increase in interest expenditures on foreign debt – by 153 per cent in 1993 – could have been even higher had it not been for declining interest rates abroad and a relatively slow nominal depreciation of the Turkish lira until mid-1993. Altogether, the share of interest expenditures in total budget expenditures grew from 18 per cent in 1992 to 24 per cent in 1993.

Personnel expenditures rose by 77.5 per cent as a result of the semi-annual adjustment in civil servants' salaries to higher-than-projected inflation in line

Table 11. Central government budget

TL trillion

	1990	1991	1992	1993 Programme	1993 Estimate	1994 Programme	1990	1991	1992	1993 Estimate	1994 Programme[1]
							Percentage change over previous year				
Revenues	55.2	96.7	174.2	344.4	360.2	627.0	81.8	75.1	80.1	106.8	74.1
Tax revenues	45.4	78.6	141.6	243.6	265.2	473.0	77.7	73.2	80.2	87.3	78.4
Direct taxes	23.7	41.1	71.4	119.0	127.8	216.7	73.4	73.7	73.7	79.0	69.6
Indirect taxes	21.7	37.6	70.2	124.6	137.4	256.3	82.6	72.7	86.7	95.7	86.5
Non-tax revenues	7.5	8.7	29.5	97.9	91.0	148.0	76.4	15.7	239.0	208.5	62.6
Grants	1.6	8.4	1.7	0.9	2.0	3.0	1 325.9	415.7	–80.0	17.6	50.0
Annex budget	0.7	0.9	1.4	2.0	2.0	3.0	50.6	42.9	55.5	42.9	50.0
Expenditures	67.2	130.3	221.7	397.7	482.2	819.0	76.6	93.9	70.1	117.5	69.8
Personnel expenditures	26.5	49.3	94.1	145.0	167.0	265.0	111.1	86.3	90.9	77.5	58.7
Other current expenditures	6.9	11.1	20.1	35.0	37.7	68.5	70.0	60.7	81.1	87.6	81.7
Interest payments	14.0	24.1	40.3	73.0	117.4	217.5	69.1	72.4	67.2	191.1	85.3
Foreign borrowing	4.4	7.1	9.8	20.0	24.8	39.0	38.4	63.8	38.0	153.1	57.3
Domestic borrowing	9.6	16.9	30.5	53.0	92.6	178.5	87.9	76.2	80.5	203.6	93.2
Investment	8.9	17.2	29.2	47.0	54.0	86.0	75.7	92.6	70.7	84.9	59.3
Transfers to SEEs	1.3	12.2	8.1	20.0	25.2	38.0	2.4	873.7	–33.6	209.9	51.4
Other transfers	9.7	16.5	29.9	77.7	80.8	144.0	40.6	69.7	81.2	170.2	78.2
Budget balance	–12.0	–33.5	–47.5	–53.3	–122.0	–192.0					
Primary balance	2.0	–9.4	–7.1	19.7	–4.6	25.5					
Deferred payments	1.2	3.6	0.8	–	–	–					
Advanced payments[2]	–1.6	–3.5	11.2	–	–	–					
Cash balance	–12.4	–33.4	–59.4	–53.3	–122.0	–192.0					
Memorandum items (per cent of GNP):											
Revenues	19.2	21.3	22.4	28.1	27.2	29.4					
Tax revenues	15.8	17.4	18.2	19.8	20.1	22.1					
Expenditures	23.4	28.7	28.4	32.4	36.5	38.3					
Budget balance	–4.2	–7.4	–6.1	–4.3	–9.2	–9.0					
Excluding grants	–4.7	–9.2	–6.2	–4.4	–9.4	–9.1					
Cash balance	–4.3	–7.1	–7.6	–4.3	–9.2	–9.0					
Primary balance	0.7	–2.1	–0.9	1.6	–0.3	1.2					
Personnel expenditures	9.2	10.9	12.1	12.0	12.7	12.4					
Interest payments	4.9	5.3	5.1	6.1	8.9	10.2					

1. Percentage changes are based on the 1993 Budget estimates available in October 1993 when the 1994 Budget was prepared.
2. In 1992 interest payments of TL 6.4 trillion are recorded as advanced payments and budgeted in the 1993 Budget.
Source: Data provided by the Turkish authorities.

Diagram 6. **CENTRAL GOVERNMENT DEFICIT AND DEBT**

As per cent of GNP

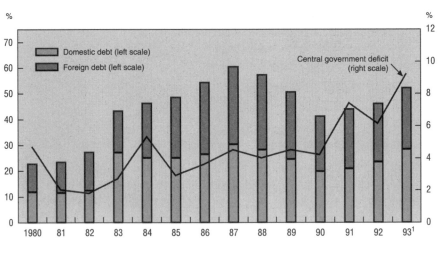

1. Estimates.
Source: Data provided by the Turkish authorities.

with the stated intention of the government that the growth in salaries would not fall below inflation. If the wage components included in investment outlays and in other transfers – wages of personnel in semi-public institutions and short-term contract workers – are also counted, the share of the total wage bill in total spending now amounts to just over 40 per cent.

Transfers from the Treasury to the SEEs through equity increases or compensation for ''duty losses'' – in addition to off-budget relief operations through an issuing of Treasury paper to meet the SEEs' debt commitments with commercial banks – remained substantial. The doubling of budget transfers to the Pension Fund Administration reflects in part the – fairly generous – early retirement scheme which came into effect in 1992.[13]

Revenues

Although central government revenues grew faster than budgeted in 1993 – by an estimated 107 per cent compared with the projected 98 per cent – as a ratio to GNP revenues are likely to have missed the target by a full percentage point. The increase in tax revenues by 87 per cent – 14 percentage points more than expected – owes largely to accelerating economic activity, but also to discretionary policy measures: in December 1992, VAT rates on luxury goods were raised from 15 to 20 per cent and the list of goods put into this category was extended. Moreover, several groups of income earners who had previously been taxed according to the "lump-sump tax system" were obliged to file an income declaration, which is likely to have raised their income tax liabilities.

For the first time since 1988, more than half of the tax revenues came from indirect taxes, boosted by inflation and booming domestic demand. Including the expected revenue-raising effect of the new VAT rates effective from 1 November 1993,[14] total VAT collection is officially estimated to have increased by nearly 93 per cent. Tax income from foreign trade grew by 97 per cent, driven by the spectacular surge in imports.

Personal income tax receipts – accounting for more than 40 per cent of total tax revenues – rose by 80 per cent, slightly more than budgeted. Despite weakened profitability of SEEs and large amounts of deferred tax payments, the outcome for corporate tax revenues exceeded budget projections, partly due to a regulation introduced in 1992 which set a floor of 23 per cent to the *effective* corporate tax rate – half of the statutory rate – after accounting for all tax exemptions. However, the corporate tax/GNP ratio remained at a low 1.2 per cent in 1993; in the mid-1980s it was around 2.2 per cent.

Latest official estimates for non-tax revenues do not differ significantly from the initial projections. However, part of the recorded surge in non-tax revenues in 1993 was a result of book-keeping operations: the Treasury retained TL 6.2 trillion as revenue out of the TL 25 trillion recorded as "transfers to SEEs" in the budget – to compensate for unpaid debt of SEEs to the Treasury. Moreover, the more-than-threefold increase in non-tax revenues estimated for 1993 is hard to reconcile with actual developments known so far (Table 12). First, doubt can be raised as to how EBFs' revenues (TL 35 trillion during the first 9 months of the year) can leap to a level of TL 64.5 trillion. Second, efforts to speed up the privatisation of SEEs notwithstanding, it is far from clear how the estimated revenues of TL 8.0 trillion can be realised in 1993 (after only TL 0.5 trillion in 1992 and TL 0.9 trillion in the first 11 months of 1993).

Table 12. Central government budget revenues

TL trillion

	1989	1990	1991	1992	1993 Programme	1993 Estimate	1994 Programme	Percentage change over previous year					
								1989	1990	1991	1992	1993 Estimate	1994 Programme [1]
Taxes on income	13.5	23.3	40.4	70.1	117.0	124.3	212.5	94.7	72.6	73.9	73.5	77.3	70.6
Personal income tax	9.9	18.6	33.4	60.0	102.0	107.8	185.0	105.6	88.5	79.2	79.6	79.7	71.6
Corporate income tax	3.6	4.6	7.1	10.1	15.0	16.5	27.5	69.9	28.9	52.3	42.2	63.4	66.6
Taxes on wealth	0.2	0.4	0.7	1.3	2.0	2.5	4.2	19.8	132.9	64.6	85.7	92.5	68.0
Taxes on goods and services	7.6	13.7	24.7	47.4	84.3	92.9	172.3	70.3	78.9	80.6	91.9	95.6	85.5
Taxes on foreign trade	4.2	8.1	12.9	22.8	40.3	45.5	83.6	58.9	89.8	59.7	76.7	99.6	83.7
Total tax revenues	25.6	45.4	78.6	141.6	243.6	265.2	473.0	79.5	77.7	73.2	80.2	87.3	78.5
Non-tax regular revenues	2.5	3.9	4.0	8.2	18.6	18.5	26.0						
Privatisation revenues	0	0.4	0	0.5	7.5	8.0	30.0						
Special revenues and funds [2]	1.8	3.3	4.8	21.9	71.8	64.5	92.0						
Grants	0.1	1.6	8.4	1.7	0.9	2.0	3.0						
Total non-tax revenues	4.4	9.2	17.2	31.2	98.8	93.0	151.0	75.4	109.1	87.0	97.7	173.5	62.4
Annex budget revenues	0.4	0.7	0.9	1.4	2.0	2.0	3.0	56.0	50.8	42.8	55.6	0	50.0
Total consolidated budget revenues	30.4	55.2	96.7	174.2	344.4	360.2	627.0	78.5	81.8	75.1	80.1	106.8	74.1

1. Percentage changes are based on the 1993 Budget estimates available in October 1993 when the 1994 Budget was prepared.
2. Including transfers from EBFs.
Source: Data provided by the Ministry of Finance.

The 1994 central government budget

The 1994 budget programme has been drawn up on the assumptions of 4.5 per cent GNP growth, average (GNP) inflation of 54 per cent, a 72 per cent average interest rate, a current external deficit of 3.5 per cent of GNP and a nominal depreciation *vis-à-vis* US dollar of about 65 per cent, which implies 6 per cent real depreciation. Given this scenario, which may have become unrealistic by the events in foreign exchange and financial markets in January 1994, the budget envisages a rising share of both expenditures and revenues in GNP by about 2 percentage points, thereby keeping the 1994 consolidated budget deficit at 9 per cent of GNP, the estimated outturn for 1993. The primary budget balance is expected to swing from a small deficit into a surplus of 1.2 per cent of GNP.

Overall expenditures are projected to grow at a rate of 70 per cent, which implies a marked slowdown. The total wage bill – including salary provisions in investment expenditures and in transfers – is set to increase by under 59 per cent so that its share in total budget outlays would fall from above 40 per cent in 1993 to 37 per cent in 1994. In addition to tighter wage policy, personnel expenditures are contained through the establishment of wage budgets per spending agency, which impose ceilings on the total expenditures for seasonal work and overtime compensation. Also, the employers' and employees' contributions to the wage-earners' compulsory saving scheme have been halved. Moreover, the municipalities' personnel expenditures are now subjected to the approval of the Ministry of the Interior.

TL 217.5 trillion are appropriated for interest payments, corresponding to 26 per cent of total budget spending and 10 per cent of GNP. However, the strong increase in interest rates in the wake of the January 1994 foreign exchange market crisis is likely to induce interest payments in excess of budget estimates. The rising share of interest payments in the budget is crowding out other expenditures. The trend decline of investment's weight in the budget – from over 20 per cent in the mid-1980s to around 10 per cent at present – is expected to continue. In line with past years' practice, investment expenditures are in general allocated to projects already under way and a large component of this budget item is actually dedicated to wage payments. The share in total budget appropriations of expenditures devoted to education is also to decrease by about 2 percentage points to 15½ per cent in 1994. The declining relative importance of both investment and education expenditures is indicative of the ongoing narrowing of the government's options with respect to resource allocation.

A large part of the TL 144 trillion of "other transfers" goes to EBFs (TL 51 trillion), the Agricultural Bank for agricultural subsidies (TL 12 trillion for cotton and fertilisers) and the Pension Fund Administration. On the other hand, appropriations for wage-earners' tax rebates are halved as a result of a move towards the eventual abolition of the rebate system.[15] Payments under this scheme will be confined to retired civil servants only and will be made at the end of the calendar year instead of every month. The rise in other current expenditures is mainly due to additional military spending.

The growth of tax revenues is projected to slow down in line with the assumed deceleration of nominal GNP. The main contribution to the increase in tax revenues is expected to come from indirect taxes, in particular value-added tax and the petroleum consumption tax. The recent tax measures will only partially support budget revenues in 1994, as the bulk of the changes are related to personal income and corporate tax, the revenues of which will be affected in full only in 1995 (see the section on structural reform below).

The realisation of the budget is subject to considerable risk. The final deficit in 1993 could exceed the current official estimate of 9.2 per cent of GNP. Moreover, on the expenditure side of the 1994 budget, projections for personnel spending and interest payments crucially depend on whether inflation and interest rates can actually be brought down to target levels. With the government's claims on resources remaining very high, and unabated recourse to monetary financing, it is unclear what mechanisms are in place to bring about lower inflation in 1994.

On the revenue side, there is the risk that indirect tax revenues might suffer from increased tax evasion as a possible consequence of higher VAT rates on basic goods, combined with the gradual phasing out of the tax rebate scheme; the latter was introduced to enforce correct accounting practices in retail trade and thereby fight tax evasion. However, preliminary data after the VAT rate increase in November 1993 suggest buoyant revenues from VAT. A substantial downside risk also exists in non-tax revenue projections (TL 151 trillion, one-fourth of total revenues), which originate primarily from revenue contributions of EBFs (TL 92 trillion) and from privatisation. To achieve the projected budget revenues from privatisation of TL 30 trillion[16] in 1994, after a very optimistic official estimate of TL 8 trillion for 1993, would require a major breakthrough in the privatisation process.

Financing the central-government deficit

In the initial budget financing programme for 1993 the government intended to draw primarily on domestic markets and to shift financial instruments towards longer maturities so as to achieve net repayment of short-term Treasury bills. This plan did not materialise owing to the large cash deficit inherited from the 1992 budget, reluctance of markets to accept the longer-term instruments offered by the Treasury at existing yields and the much higher-than-planned borrowing requirement. Hence, as in earlier years domestic borrowing concentrated on Treasury bills, and net long-term borrowing – mostly one-year government bonds – turned out to be only half of the amount envisaged in the programme. Altogether, borrowing from domestic markets financed some 60 per cent of the deficit in 1993, a decline from the 66 per cent recorded in 1992 (Table 13).

The Treasury therefore continued to rely heavily on Central Bank credits; current estimates suggest that about one-third of the deficit has been funded by Central Bank credits in 1993. In the summer of 1993, when the Treasury reached the legal limit[17] of Central Bank short-term advances for budget financing, TL 13.5 trillion of Central Bank credits to the Treasury were consolidated against special government bonds with a maturity of 10 years and 20 per cent interest rate. Moreover, the supplementary budget approved in November 1993 raised the amount of central government budget appropriations and hence increased the volume of Central Bank funds at the disposal of the government.

International sources also had to be tapped by more than planned in order to bridge the financing gap, so that the share of net foreign borrowing in deficit financing may have been as high as $6\frac{1}{2}$ per cent in 1993, rather than the initially projected $2\frac{1}{2}$ per cent; it was negative during the late 1980s.

The pattern of financing of the deficit envisaged for 1994 is broadly similar to that of 1993, with the exception of foreign credit. The authorities plan to cut the net foreign borrowing to almost nil from 6 per cent of total deficit in 1993. Recourse to the Central Bank sources will remain roughly unchanged at 33 per cent of the deficit and 2 per cent of GNP. With regard to domestic borrowing, the Treasury intends to continue the gradual shift, under way since mid-1993,

Table 13. **Financing of the budget deficit**

TL trillion

	1990	1991	1992	1993 Programme	1993 Estimate	1994 Programme
Cash balance	−12.4	−33.4	−59.4	−53.3	−122.0	−192.0
Financing						
Central Bank, net	0.3	10.7	17.4	27.0	39.0	63.7
Foreign borrowing	0.0	1.9	4.0	1.3	8.1	1.0
Receipts	5.5	10.9	19.7	22.4	31.8	45.7
Repayments	−5.5	−9.0	−15.7	21.1	−23.7	−44.7
Domestic borrowing, net	12.0	20.8	38.0	25.0	74.9	127.3
Government bonds [1]	8.0	2.3	15.4	49.0	20.5	26.5
Receipts	12.5	11.5	35.6	95.0	55.2	99.6
Repayments	−4.6	−9.2	−20.2	−46.0	−34.7	−73.1
Treasury bills [2]	1.9	12.8	24.0	−24.0	54.4	100.8
Receipts	8.4	34.3	75.9	8.6	203.3	289.9
Repayments	−6.5	−21.5	−51.9	−32.6	−148.9	−189.1
Other borrowing [3]	2.1	5.7	−1.4	–	–	–
As per cent of cash balance						
Central Bank	2.5	32.0	29.3	50.7	32.0	33.2
Foreign borrowing	0	5.7	6.7	2.4	6.6	0.5
Domestic borrowing, net	97.5	62.3	64.0	46.9	61.4	66.3
Government bonds	64.5	6.9	26.0	91.9	16.8	13.8
Treasury Bills	15.3	38.3	40.4	−45.0	44.6	52.5
Other borrowing	17.7	17.1	−2.4	–	–	–

1. 12 months and longer maturities.
2. Three, six and nine months maturities.
3. Change in bank deposits. Including errors and omissions.
Source: Data provided by the Turkish authorities.

towards longer maturities – 6 and 9 months and eventually 12 months and longer maturities.

Sustainability of government financial positions

Large and widening fiscal deficits should eventually lead to an unsustainable situation. So far, however, snowballing of debt has not occurred. From a recent trough of 43 per cent of GNP in 1990 the general government debt has continued to rise, reaching about 55 per cent of GNP at the end of 1993. Both domestic and external components of government debt increased. The volume of domestic debt rose from 20 per cent of GNP in 1990 to an estimated 30 per cent in 1993. Domestic debt includes as non-securitised debt short-term Central Bank advances to the Treasury and the accumulated exchange rate depreciation losses on net foreign liabilities of the Central Bank. When these two items are excluded the domestic debt stock only amounted to about 18 per cent of GNP in 1993. Levels of both overall debt and domestic debt are still below the OECD average.

In recent years, the composition of debt has shifted progressively towards the short end: in the summer of 1993, 65 per cent of the securitised debt stock was of less than 12 months' maturity. Hence, even though the level of domestic debt is not particularly high, the need to roll over a large share of the total debt stock almost continuously exerts pressure on the still relatively narrow financial markets.

The main reason for the relatively modest levels of debt in Turkey in spite of persistently large deficits is that, although market interest rates are high, the necessary condition for "explosive" debt growth – a real interest rate on government debt higher than real output growth – does not hold. Owing to the large share of monetary deficit financing, the effective nominal interest rate on government debt is currently of the order of 35 to 40 per cent, *i.e.* it is strongly negative in real terms.

The large share of monetary deficit financing, on the other hand, means that it is difficult to rein in inflation and hence bring down nominal interest rates. Thus, instead of snowballing of debt, Turkey has been experiencing what might be called "interest payments explosion": the budget overrun caused by higher interest payments (and higher wage bills) feeds higher inflation and interest rates. This tendency may have been accentuated by the phenomenon of currency substitution which reduces the base for inflation tax (see below for the discussion of currency substitution). As noted, the share of interest payments in total government expenditure has been rising rapidly (and is expected to be 26 per cent in 1994), thereby constraining the scope for attaining desired goals through public spending.

State economic enterprises

A dramatic worsening of the financial accounts of the non-financial SEEs[18] in 1991 (Table 14) led to the government's decision to implement a rescue operation through debt consolidation at the beginning of 1992. Thereby, the SEEs' accumulated debt to social security institutions, the Treasury and the Central Bank, and tax arrears were written off, easing the SEEs' financial burden

Table 14. **Financial account of the non-financial State economic enterprises** [1]

TL billion

	1990	1991	1992	1993 Programme	1993 Estimate	1994 Programme
Operating revenues	81 554	134 309	234 204	356 667	379 160	621 892
Operating expenses	84 150	160 436	280 577	391 359	437 666	684 601
of which: Wages and salaries	16 158	35 067	57 486	90 746	98 248	156 817
Interest payments	4 569	11 237	22 518	22 832	37 682	48 737
Operating surplus	−2 596	−26 127	−46 373	−34 692	−58 506	−62 709
Direct tax payments	1 192	1 644	2 361	4 905	3 200	4 983
Income after taxes	−3 788	−27 771	−48 734	−39 597	−61 706	−67 692
Other funds available	8 673	21 941	28 892	31 200	31 462	46 299
Total funds available	4 885	−5 830	−19 842	−8 397	−30 244	−21 393
Investment expenditures	23 362	30 292	39 149	51 646	64 850	99 841
of which: Fixed investment	10 028	14 576	22 692	26 113	33 926	53 055
Changes in stocks	12 908	13 931	15 371	22 757	27 344	44 973
Gross financing requirement	−18 477	−36 122	−58 991	−60 043	−95 094	−121 234
Transfers from budget	1 749	12 537	9 749	22 620	32 888	43 775
Financing requirement	−16 728	−23 585	−49 242	−37 423	−62 206	−77 459
Deferred payments	13 034	25 068	61 427	44 034	58 965	102 235
Advance payments	−4 436	−12 398	−12 229	−8 118	−14 997	−24 818
Cash finance requirement	−8 130	−10 915	−44	−1 507	−18 238	−42
Financing						
Foreign borrowing, net	2 391	−241	2 413	−1 715	−1 174	−2 524
Loans	7 010	6 794	9 077	10 241	18 498	18 588
Repayments	−4 619	−7 035	−6 664	−11 956	−19 672	−21 112
Domestic bank lending, net	5 900	11 022	2 940	982	16 874	3 440
Central Bank	0	3 829	−731	0	10 810	8 605
State Investment Bank (Eximbank)	142	−11	−339	−173	−240	−109
Commercial banks	5 758	7 204	4 010	1 155	6 304	−5 056
Change in cash/bank	−161	134	−5 309	2 240	2 538	−873
Memorandum items						
Operating surplus/operating revenues	−3.2	−19.5	−19.8	−9.7	−15.4	−10.1
Financing requirement/GNP	−5.8	−5.2	−6.3	−3.1	−4.7	−3.6
Excluding budget transfers	−6.4	−8.0	−7.6	−4.9	−7.2	−5.6

1. Including the State economic enterprises in the process of privatisation.
Source: Data provided by the State Planning Organisation and the Under-Secretariat of the Treasury and Foreign Trade.

by TL 25.7 trillion in 1992. Moreover, the SEEs were provided with TL 14.5 trillion additional off-budget financing facilities in the form of government securities to repay debt to social security institutions and arrears on commercial loans. On account of the expected amelioration in their financial structure after the debt relief operation, the SEEs' financing requirement had initially been hoped to fall to 3.3 per cent of GNP in 1992. However, recently revised financial accounts for 1992 indicate a much stronger expenditure growth than estimated earlier, due in particular to higher-than-expected interest payments. Accordingly, the SEEs' financing requirement for 1992 had to be revised upward to 6.3 per cent of GNP, the highest since the late 1970s, in spite of the sizeable debt relief.

Preliminary estimates for 1993 suggest that the growth of the (non-financial) SEEs' operating expenditures slowed down by nearly 20 percentage points to 55 per cent while their revenues rose by 62 per cent, thereby lowering the operating loss from 20.0 per cent of revenues in 1992 to 15.4 per cent in 1993. The growth of interest payments declined, but not by as much as projected, while the growth of personnel expenditures accelerated to 71 per cent in 1993, reflecting the compensation for the high inflation of 1992 by new collective wage agreements.[19] Fixed investment appears to have fallen in real terms, but the destocking observed in 1992 came to a halt. Inventory accumulation in agricultural SEEs, notably in the Monopoly Administration, Soil Products Office (TMO) and the Sugar Corporation – more than 80 per cent of total SEE stocks – started picking up in early 1993, partly owing to increases in agricultural support prices. The resulting gross financing requirement – before budget transfers – remained almost unchanged in relation to GNP, around 7¼ per cent in 1993.

The Monopoly Administration (TEKEL) ran the largest deficit in 1993, accounting for about one fourth of the financing requirement. Other SEEs incurring large deficits were the National Railways, TMO, the Sugar Corporation and the Iron and Steel Industry which together made up another 40 per cent of the total financing need.

The recorded decrease in the SEEs' net deficit by 1½ percentage points to 4¾ per cent of GNP in 1993 is the result of various injections from the central government. Transfers from the government budget were particularly high in 1993, about 3.6 per cent of GNP. The Coal Industry, the National Railways, TMO, the Iron and Steel Industry, the Sugar Corporation and TEKEL alone received nearly 80 per cent of total budget transfers. Moreover, the SEEs were again given off-budget aid in the form of government bonds (about TL 15 trillion in 1993) as well as implicit transfers through unpaid debt obligations (labelled as "deferred payments"), which have become a regular practice of "financing" the SEE deficit. Deferred payments customarily include corporate tax arrears, excise taxes retained by the Monopoly Administration and borrowing from EBFs.[20] In 1993, net deferred payments – after allowing for advances extended to farmers and contractors – covered 70 per cent of the SEEs' borrowing requirement; in 1992, this ratio was almost 100 per cent. When off-budget aid and implicit transfers are included, the so derived true Treasury financing of SEEs amounts to about 6 per cent of GNP in 1993. In 1992 it even reached 10 per cent of GNP, after inclusion of the SEEs' net gain from the government's debt relief operation. Another worrying feature of SEE financing is that the TMO was again admitted access to Central Bank sources in 1993, after the interruption of this practice in 1992.

The programme for 1994 has been prepared on the basis of incomplete data for 1993, which are likely to be substantially revised. It foresees a reduction in the operating loss to 10 per cent of operating revenues. It is hoped that this will be brought about mainly by faster growth of operating revenues. The wage bill is expected to grow by 60 per cent, which may be realistic. The projection of only 30 per cent increase in interest payments is hard to assess as it is net of transfers from the central government budget; such accounting practice is clearly in conflict with the principle of transparency. Altogether, the 1994 financing requirement of SEEs is programmed to be cut back by 1 percentage point to 3.6 per cent of GNP.

Privatisation

In addition to the privatisation projects in process at the Public Participation Administration (PPA), in principle the sole body in charge of privatisation,[21] a new approach was tried at the end of 1992: selected SEEs were to become directly responsible for their own restructuring and privatisation, thereby by-passing the PPA. The new procedure was applied first to the Sümerbank, whose banking and manufacturing sections were split into independent units. Assets and liabilities of the banking section were taken over by the Treasury. However, the authority for privatisation granted by a government decree to PTT has been countermanded by the Constitutional Court on account of the decree's nonconformity with existing legislation. Efforts are currently being made by the government to amend the legal basis for the new approach. At the same time, preparations have been completed for the restructuring of the PTT through detaching its telephone section and establishing it as an independent Telephone Corporation. The government's plan is to sell at least 10 to 20 per cent of the latter's shares in 1994. It is also envisaged to separate the electricity distribution part from TEK.

The PPA sold four cement factories, a supermarket chain, a road vehicle manufacturer as well as minority share holdings of variety of companies in 1993. But largely due to diverse legal and political obstacles, the progress achieved in the privatisation programme fell much behind initial expectations. By early November, the privatisation revenues totalled $376 million as compared to the $1.5 billion programmed for the whole year. In addition to TEK and PTT, currently listed for privatisation are PETKIM (petrochemical industry), the Petroleum Office, Turkish Airways, TURBAN (hotels and tourism), TÜPRAS (refineries), TOPAS (mainly automobiles), the Maritime transport company and some small agro-industry enterprises, altogether accounting for almost one-third of the aggregate SEE revenues in 1993.

Monetary conditions determined by government financing requirements

Large and growing government financing requirements have continued to inhibit the conduct of monetary policy. As a prerequisite for controlling money supply, the Central Bank established in 1990 a medium-term strategy which aimed at controlling the volume and structure of its own balance sheet.[22] Annual monetary programmes were formulated on the basis of this strategy.[23] Key assumptions for the 1992 monetary programme were a consolidated government budget deficit of no more than TL 32 trillion (4½ per cent of projected GNP) and the public sector's borrowing from the Central Bank not exceeding TL 11 trillion. However, already in the early months of 1992, the Treasury had used up all of the Central Bank credits envisaged for the whole year so that compliance with the targets of the annual monetary programme became illusory. In the event, Central Bank money grew by about 100 per cent, twice as much as targeted under the 1992 programme (Table 15).

Table 15. Assets and liabilities of the Central Bank.

End of period	TL trillion		As per cent of total				Percentage change over corresponding period at previous year			1993			
	1992	1993	1990	1991	1992	1993	1990	1991	1992	Q1	Q2	Q3	Q4[1]
Assets	177.2	285.8	100.0	100.0	100.0	100.0	24.5	58.7	83.1	81.9	64.8	61.6	61.3
Foreign assets	75.7	128.1	41.9	40.0	42.7	44.8	42.5	51.4	95.6	127.9	110.1	81.1	69.2
Domestic assets	101.5	157.7	58.1	60.0	57.3	55.2	-8.5	184.8	160.5	97.9	73.4	48.0	55.4
Credits	66.7	125.7	14.8	26.5	37.7	44.0	-2.3	164.9	155.5	97.3	73.8	86.1	88.5
Public sector	62.6	108.5	8.7	23.7	35.3	38.0	-33.2	330.1	173.3	92.7	67.3	84.0	73.3
Banking sector	9.4	18.7	8.7	5.0	5.3	6.5	75.5	-0.5	78.3	129.8	127.2	117.0	99.0
Other items, net	-5.3	-1.5	-2.7	-2.7	-3.0	-0.5	55.7	56.3	105.6	87.8	82.8	128.2	-72.0
Devaluation account	34.8	31.9	43.3	33.5	19.6	11.2	24.3	22.8	7.1	-6.2	-15.9	-14.0	-8.3
Liabilities	177.2	285.8	100.0	100.0	100.0	100.0	24.5	58.7	83.1	81.9	64.8	61.6	61.3
Foreign currency liabilities	89.4	157.8	60.9	54.5	50.4	55.2	21.9	42.1	69.3	72.7	56.2	56.2	76.5
– to non-residents	61.3	111.1	42.8	40.9	34.6	38.9	26.0	46.7	60.0	63.3	60.1	67.1	81.2
– to residents	28.1	46.6	18.1	14.9	15.8	16.3	12.4	31.2	94.1	96.2	47.6	33.0	65.8
FX deposits (non-bank)	10.8	16.7	7.6	5.4	6.1	5.8	-3.6	13.8	106.0	132.3	37.0	12.0	54.6
FX deposits at banks	17.3	29.9	10.5	9.5	9.7	10.5	25.7	43.7	88.0	74.1	56.8	49.0	72.8
TL liabilities (Central Bank money)	87.8	128.1	39.1	45.5	49.6	44.8	28.8	84.6	99.7	92.2	74.9	67.2	45.9
Currency issues	36.8	63.1	23.1	22.0	20.8	22.1	68.2	51.3	73.0	82.5	77.9	86.4	71.5
Banks' deposits	23.1	36.0	14.6	14.6	13.0	12.6	14.3	59.3	63.3	63.8	54.8	38.1	56.5
Other Central Bank money	27.9	29.0	1.4	8.8	15.7	10.1	-63.3	877.0	228.2	139.1	88.6	67.0	3.9

1. Provisional.
Source: Central Bank of Turkey, Quarterly Bulletin.

As a consequence of these developments, the Central Bank abstained from formulating a monetary programme for 1993, leaving financial markets with little guidance about the Bank's policy strategy. Instead, it appears that monetary developments in 1993 have once again been dominated by the government's financing requirements, while the Central Bank has focused its attention on maintaining orderly conditions in the money and foreign-exchange market. In particular, open market sales were undertaken by the Bank to prevent excess liquidity from putting pressures on the foreign exchange market.

The monetary authorities' ability to maintain orderly financial market conditions were put to a severe test in the second half of January 1994: the downgrading of Turkey's credit rating by two leading rating agencies apparently triggered a run on the lira, against the background of ongoing efforts of the Treasury to bring interest rates on government securities down and the heavy Central Bank financing of public deficits. As a result, the Turkish lira depreciated temporarily up to nearly 30 per cent. When the Central Bank mopped up abundant liquidity through open-market operations, money market interest rates were driven up and the loss in the lira's external value was reduced to some 13 per cent.

In late January 1994, government and Central Bank unveiled a package of measures to further stabilise the currency. Major elements of the package were an increase in the discount rate from 48 to 56 per cent, a rise in the interest rate on cash advances to banks from the Central Bank from 54.5 to 65 per cent and the abolition of the 5 per cent transactions tax on bonds and on repo transactions, which had been introduced only at the beginning of 1994. The legal reserve requirement and the liquidity ratio were unified to a single "liquidity requirement ratio" and its coverage extended to non-deposit liabilities.[24] The combined effect of the measures was upward pressure on market interest rates: for example, one-year deposit rates jumped from 75 to over 90 per cent and three-months Treasury bill rates from around 70 to some 100 per cent in early February 1994.

Money and credit

Central Bank credits to the banking system, which were depressed in 1991 and in the first half of 1992, recovered in the second half of 1992 and further during 1993, largely mirroring urgent financing needs of the agricultural sector, but also reflecting buoyant economic activity. As explained below, however, lending by deposit money banks, which currently account for more than three-quarters of total domestic credit, grew even more rapidly than this, nearly doubling during 1993 (Table 16). In particular, consumer credits, which were virtually non-existent before 1990, grew at a rate of nearly 200 per cent during 1993, reaching a share of about 7 per cent in credits extended to the private sector. The growth of Central Bank lending to the public sector slowed in 1993 relative to the extraordinary expansion in 1991 and 1992, though it remained high. The slow-

Table 16. **Money and credit**

End of period	1992	1993 September [1]	1990	1991	1992	1993 Q1	1993 Q2	1993 Q3 [1]
	TL trillion		Percentage change over corresponding period of previous year					
Reserve money	61.2	92.4	40.1	56.0	64.3	73.1	69.6	68.3
Currency in circulation	30.4	48.0	66.3	52.6	74.7	78.8	78.2	79.1
Sight deposits	48.0	58.7	57.4	46.5	63.5	82.5	85.6	73.2
M1	78.4	106.7	60.5	49.0	63.5	82.5	85.6	75.7
Time deposits	112.4	135.7	45.9	75.0	59.7	56.7	44.0	35.8
M2	190.8	242.4	51.8	63.0	61.9	65.2	57.7	50.9
Foreign exchange deposits	103.2	155.4	54.2	227.5	102.7	86.2	62.2	58.1
M2X	294.0	397.8	52.3	81.0	75.0	72.2	59.4	53.6
Domestic credits	244.4	370.4	71.3	75.2	86.9	78.7	85.9	102.6[3]
by: Deposit banks	185.4	294.7	71.3	75.1	82.7	85.2	95.1	103.1
Investment banks	16.4	21.6	41.1	117.3	50.8	48.9	65.0	63.6
Central Bank [2]	42.6	54.2	28.0	314.3	130.7	65.4	57.2	117.6[3]
to: Treasury	43.8	55.8	21.0	215.5	116.2	63.8	59.4	169.6[3]
Public enterprises	17.0	26.3	92.1	70.6	33.5	24.1	41.4	35.5
Private sector	181.7	284.4	76.7	61.9	88.8	90.7	85.9	104.9
Local governments	2.3	3.9	33.9	53.8	97.9	77.9	100.0	116.6
			Percentage distribution					
Domestic credits			100.0	100.0	100.0	100.0	100.0	100.0
by: Deposit banks			87.3	77.6	75.9	76.3	77.9	79.6
Investment banks			6.7	8.3	6.7	6.3	5.6	5.8
Central Bank [2]			6.0	14.1	17.4	17.4	16.5	14.6
to: Treasury			8.1	14.5	16.8	17.2	16.4	15.1
Public enterprises			11.1	10.8	7.7	7.2	7.9	7.1
Private sector			79.8	73.7	74.5	74.8	74.8	76.8
Local governments			1.0	0.9	0.9	0.9	1.0	1.0

1. Provisional.
2. Excluding Central Bank credits to banking sector.
3. In August 1993, TL 21.3 trillion of the Central Bank credits to the public sector (TL 13.5 to the Treasury and TL 7.8 trillion to the Soil Products Office [TMO]) were consolidated. Above figures for the percentage changes in the third quarter of 1993 include consolidated credits.
Source: Central Bank of Turkey, *Quarterly Bulletin.*

down in lending to the government was largely associated with a reduced pace of direct loans extended to the Treasury,[25] reflecting the government's stronger recourse to the issuance of Treasury bills and government bonds. The latter have been sold not only directly to the public, but also on a large scale to the Central Bank as the existing stock of government bonds held by the Central Bank for the purpose of open market operations was deemed inadequate.

The strong growth of bank credits to the private sector is not commensurately reflected in the development of reserve money[26] in 1993, which expanded broadly in line with developments a year earlier. More strikingly, the growth of CBM[27] decelerated in the course of 1993, which – if taken at face value – would signal improved Central Bank control of monetary aggregates. For instance, one of the targets of the Central Bank's medium-term programme of 1990 was to keep the rate of growth of the Bank's balance sheet below the growth rate of nominal GNP, a target which is estimated to have been achieved in 1993. However, the diverging growth paths of bank credits and reserve money are a consequence of financial market reform in 1992, which legalised the existing practice of repurchase (''repo'') transactions[28] and which permitted the securitisation of assets, thereby allowing financial institutions to collect non-deposit funds which are not subject to (non-interest bearing) legal or liquidity reserve holdings with the Central Bank.

Another reported widespread technique of bank funding is the transfer of Turkish lira abroad and subsequent borrowing in the form of foreign exchange loans, transactions which have been facilitated by the convertibility of the Turkish lira and financial market liberalisation. This new technique is highly cost saving for banks as it not only avoids the holding of required reserves on bank deposits, but also allows the tax deductibility of losses arising from the appreciation of foreign-currency denominated liabilities, while corresponding capital gains are not subject to taxation. Altogether, as in other OECD countries, financial market reform in Turkey has – at least temporarily – made the evaluation of monetary conditions through the monitoring of monetary aggregates very difficult, if not impossible.

The rapid increase in the monetary aggregate M1 during 1993 bears witness to the strength of economic growth. At the same time, the expansion of M2 slowed somewhat as Turkish lira time deposits seem to have been progressively converted into higher-yielding government securities[29] and foreign currency deposits. The latter protect the depositor against Turkish lira depreciation and have provided for fairly attractive interest rates in recent years. Hence, M2X, conventional M2 plus (the domestic currency value of) foreign-exchange deposits of Turkish residents, displayed a rather dynamic development, particularly in 1992 but also in 1993. The rising share of the foreign-exchange component in M2X[30] has given rise to concern about increasing currency substitution in Turkey and its potential adverse consequences (see below).

Interest and exchange rates

As a consequence of the Treasury's decision to meet its financing needs through stronger recourse to bond sales at the expense of three-month Treasury bills, short-term interest rates declined gradually from their peak levels attained in the second and third quarter of 1992. On the other hand, rates on long-term bonds – which in the Turkish context regularly means a maturity of one year only – rose from their temporary trough of 72 per cent in early 1992 to 87 per cent by the summer of 1993 (Table 17). Consequent upon measures to stabilise the Turkish lira exchange rate in late January 1994, interest rates of all maturities rose sharply.

The real return on risk-free government bonds (deflated by the consumer price index), which was negative for all maturities during most of 1990, turned out extraordinarily high[31] in 1992 and 1993. For a maturity of one year, real bond rates were above 13 per cent during the first half of 1993, suggesting the prevalence of very tight monetary conditions. Such real bond rate levels leave little doubt that business investment is being crowded out by government borrowing, an observation which finds support from the reported high share (some 25 per cent) of interest income in total private business net value-added in 1992 in the sample of the Istanbul Chamber of Industry. "Non-preferential" (*i.e.* not subsidised) lending rates, for which no official statistics are available, are reported to have stood at a level of above 100 per cent. The implied real credit interest rates clearly represent a substantial obstacle to business investment, which needs a boost in preparing for the customs union with the European Community.

Apart from operating costs, provisions for bad loans and the return on equity, the wide margins between the banks' lending and borrowing rates reflects the rather complex system of taxes and levies applied to financial transactions.

Table 17. Interest rates

Per cent per annum, average annualised rates

	1990 Annual	1991 Q1	Q2	Q3	Q4	Annual	1992 Q1	Q2	Q3	Q4	Annual	1993 Q1	Q2	Q3	Q4	Annual
Nominal TL rates																
Bank deposits[1]																
Sight deposits[2]	12	12	12	12	12	12	12	11	11	11	11	11	11	11	11	11
Time deposits[2]																
3 months	64	74	76	85	91	82	87	91	85	89	88	84	81	81	78	81
6 months	56	69	72	87	83	76	81	81	80	81	81	81	81	82	82	82
1 year	58	64	62	71	73	68	72	74	74	74	74	74	75	75	75	75
Government bonds																
3 months	57	75	89	87	94	86	87	94	100	97	94	94	87	81	81	86
6 months	56	72	80	76	85	78	83	87	90	88	87	88	88	88	82	87
1 year	52	67	70	68	75	70	72	75	78	78	76	80	85	87	88	85
Real rates[3]																
Bank deposits																
3 months	2.3	7.0	7.8	9.6	13.6	9.6	4.9	12.4	11.1	12.6	5.9	16.0	10.5	6.0	5.1	9.0
6 months	-2.7	3.9	5.4	7.2	10.0	7.2	1.5	6.6	8.2	7.8	6.5	14.1	10.5	6.1	7.5	9.6
1 year	-1.5	0.9	0.7	1.3	2.9	1.2	-3.5	2.5	4.6	3.6	2.3	9.7	6.8	2.5	3.3	5.4
Government bonds																
3 months	-2.1	7.6	15.8	10.8	15.3	12.0	4.9	14.3	20.3	17.3	14.0	22.3	14.2	6.0	6.9	12.0
6 months	-2.6	5.8	10.3	4.3	10.0	7.2	2.6	10.1	14.2	12.0	10.0	18.5	14.7	10.0	7.5	12.6
1 year	-5.0	2.7	4.2	-0.4	3.9	2.4	-3.6	3.1	7.0	6.0	3.5	13.5	13.1	9.5	11.0	11.4
Memorandum items																
Foreign currency deposits																
rates (1 year)	8.7	8.7	8.7	8.7	8.7	8.7	8.3	8.0	7.5	7.6	7.9	7.5	7.6	7.6	7.6	7.6
Deutsche Marks	8.5	7.0	6.5	6.5	6.5	6.6	5.8	4.8	4.4	4.2	4.8	4.2	4.5	4.5	4.5	4.5
US dollars	8.5	7.0	6.5	6.5	6.5	6.6	5.8	4.8	4.4	4.2	4.8	4.2	4.5	4.5	11.0	4.5

1. Maximum rates, freely determined by banks.
2. Weighted averages.
3. Nominal rates are deflated by the consumer price index of the State Institute of Statistics.
Source: Central Bank of Turkey, *Quarterly Bulletin.*

51

Important elements of this system are the transactions tax on the banks' interest revenues, an interest surcharge accruing to the Resource Utilisation Fund and a stamp duty levied on the loan. In addition to these explicit taxes on banking, the (non-interest earning) required reserve and the (partly remunerable) liquidity reserve impose a substantial implicit tax on banks.[32] Table 18 provides a typical example of the most important elements of the spread between a non-preferential lending rate and an average bank deposit interest rate. Given the substantial magnitudes of the various components of the wedge, the resulting non-preferential lending rate to the borrower is more than double that paid to the depositor.

Assuming that the banks aim at a certain real rate of return on assets, the rate of inflation also drives a wedge between nominal and real rates of return. It can be shown analytically that under some simplifying assumptions, the spread between lending and borrowing rates is proportional to the rate of inflation.[33]

Table 18. **Decomposition of the cost of non-preferential bank loans**

Per cent, 1992

Average annual interest rate on TL deposits[1]	56.00
+ Implicit tax on deposit due to reserve requirement ratio of average 10 per cent	10.18
+ Implicit tax on deposit due to liquidity requirement ratio of 35 per cent	35.64
− Average interest revenues on liquidity reserve holdings[2]	18.90
= Costs of funds before explicit taxation and operational expenses	82.92
+ Stamp duty[3]	0.50
+ Financial transaction tax[4]	5.98
+ RUSF surcharge[5]	7.17
+ Operational cost[6]	6.00
= Cost of funds before provisions and return on capital	102.57
+ Bad loan provisions[7]	5.00
+ Profit margin[8]	12.00
= Minimum bank lending interest rate on "non-preferential loans"	119.57

1. Weighted interest rates of sight and time deposits, including official, commercial and saving deposits. Deposits in Turkish lira and interest rates for different type of deposits are taken from the Central Bank *Quarterly Bulletin*.
2. Assuming that 30 per cent of assets held by banks are government bonds bearing 70 per cent interest with a withholding tax of 10 per cent.
3. Stamp duty of 0.5 per cent is charged on total value of credits.
4. A rate of 5 per cent is applied to banks' credit interest earnings.
5. 6 per cent of the banks' credit earnings are levied in favour of the Resource Utilisation and Support Fund (RUSF).
6. Estimated from banks balance sheet.
7. Estimate is probably at the lower end of the unknown true value.
8. Estimate on the assumption of a 55 per cent return on equity.
Source: OECD estimates.

Diagram 7. **EXCHANGE RATE DEVELOPMENTS**

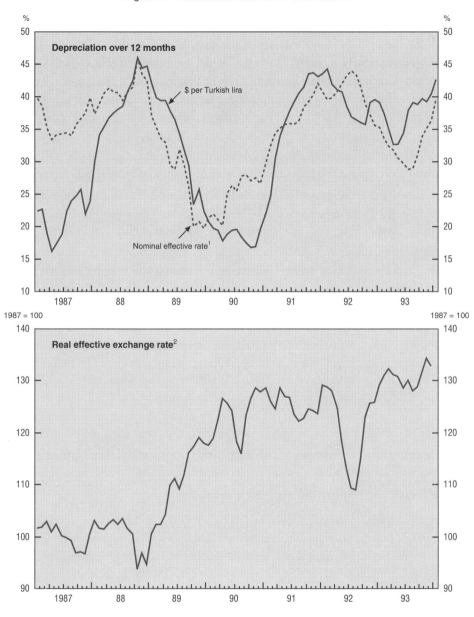

1. Trade-weighted index.
2. Ajusted for changes in consumer prices.
Source: OECD.

Hence, apart from easing the tax burden on financial intermediation, a safe way to lower the prevailing extraordinary bank spreads is to reduce inflation.

Given the persistent high inflation, the external value of the Turkish lira has been subject to steady erosion. However, when measured in real effective terms (here: trade-weighted relative consumer prices in common currency), the Turkish lira at times displays rather erratic movements, often on account of sharp fluctuations in the domestic price level. For example, when price adjustments of State Economic Enterprises caused a surge in overall inflation in early 1992, the nominal effective (trade-weighted) depreciation was insufficient to prevent a real appreciation of some $3^3/_4$ per cent.[34] This was more than offset by a sharp drop in the real exchange rate until the late summer of 1992, which was followed by another real appreciation during the remainder of the year, resulting altogether in an average annual loss in the lira's real external value by $3^1/_2$ per cent (Diagram 7).

The lira strengthened further in real terms during the first half of 1993, by some $10^1/_2$ per cent on average, as a combined result of accelerating domestic inflation and slowing nominal depreciation, the latter probably induced by the growing interest rate differential between Turkey and abroad. As in the preceding year, a correction set in later on, so that the lira ended up appreciating by some 7 per cent in real terms for 1993 on average, which is another indicator of monetary restraint. A reversal of earlier trends occurred by mid-January 1994, when the lira depreciated by some 13 per cent within a few days.

The interaction of currency substitution, seigniorage and inflation

Is there currency substitution going on ...

The strong expansion of foreign-currency deposits relative to the development of broader monetary aggregates (Diagram 8) suggests the presence of currency substitution, a process whereby foreign-currency denominated money balances increasingly replace the traditional functions of domestic money as a store of value, unit of account and medium of exchange. Strong growth of foreign currency deposits shows that foreign currency substitutes for domestic money as a store of value, probably the function of money which is most vulnerable to high inflation. However, the lack of data on foreign currency circulating in the Turkish

Diagram 8. **CURRENCY SUBSTITUTION**
Foreign currency deposits/M2X

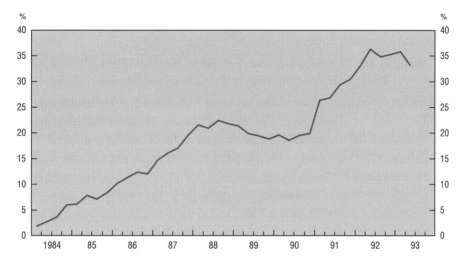

Source: OECD.

economy makes the significance of foreign money as a medium of exchange basically unobservable. Therefore the proportion of foreign exchange deposits in broader money can only be taken as an approximation of the importance of foreign currency as a means of payment. Moreover, standard empirical tests for currency substitution[35] always run the risk of not sufficiently distinguishing it from normal asset diversification, *i.e.* substitution between interest-bearing assets denominated in domestic and foreign currency.[36]

... and is it a problem?

Currency substitution is a way in which economic agents respond to a rapid erosion in the value of the Turkish lira, and in this respect it can be viewed as a form of indexation. Foreign-currency deposits may also be seen as a welcome means of raising the flow of foreign-exchange resources through formal banking channels, thereby providing some scope for alleviating external payments pressures. For example, it may well be argued that the introduction of foreign-currency deposits in Turkey in December 1983 has encouraged greater inflows of foreign exchange from migrant workers and may in certain situations also have contained capital flight. On the other hand, a substantial share of foreign currency in a monetary aggregate makes the latter's control difficult for the Central Bank because the domestic currency value of foreign exchange deposits follows any movements in the exchange rate. Moreover, foreign currency deposits are affected by transfers from abroad over which the authorities have limited control.

Another unfavourable aspect of currency substitution – especially important in the Turkish context – is related to seigniorage and the government's ability to finance fiscal deficits *via* the "inflation tax". Increased amounts of foreign currency deposits decrease the base over which the inflation tax can be levied, although this effect is attenuated by the fact that in Turkey reserve requirements are imposed on foreign exchange deposits.[37] Hence, when the public holds foreign currency, financing of a given fiscal deficit *via* the inflation tax necessitates a higher rate of inflation. A point will eventually be reached where a government finds it extremely difficult to continue to pursue inflationary deficit financing and is obliged to foster fiscal discipline.[38]

How important are seigniorage and inflation tax?

Seigniorage can be viewed as the revenue raised by the monetary authorities through issuing non-interest bearing liabilities, *i.e.* reserve money.[39] The inflation tax refers to the increase in reserve money that individuals have to accumulate to keep their real money balances constant. The difference between (monetary) seigniorage and the inflation tax owes to changes in real reserve money demand, which may be considered as the non-inflationary component of seigniorage, as it is the increase in reserve money which is compatible with a stable price level. Table 19 shows seigniorage revenues as given by the increase in reserve money divided by the same year's GNP.[40] As the table indicates, rising inflation does not necessarily generate larger seigniorage. This is so because higher levels of inflation imply rising opportunity cost of holding money which – everything else being unchanged – tends to dampen reserve money demand, thereby reducing the base of seigniorage extraction. For example, seigniorage in 1981 and 1982 exceeded that in 1980 in spite of much lower inflation.

The fact that – *ceteris paribus* – it is eminently plausible to expect seigniorage first to rise with inflation but to fall once the inflation rate has passed a certain threshold has led many to draw an analogy with the well-known "Laffer

Table 19. **Seigniorage and inflation tax**

	Consumer price inflation	Monetary seigniorage [1]	Inflation rate [2]	Opportunity cost seigniorage [3]	Opportunity cost seigniorage [4]	PSBR
				Per cent of GNP		
1974	15.8	2.9	1.4	–	–	–
1975	19.5	2.5	1.9	–	–	–
1976	17.1	2.8	1.6	–	–	–
1977	27.1	3.2	2.6	–	–	–
1978	45.3	3.8	3.9	0.7	2.5	9.5
1979	58.7	4.0	4.3	0.9	2.2	10.5
1980	110.2	2.8	6.1	1.3	2.9	10.5
1981	36.6	4.1	2.1	4.4	4.7	4.9
1982	29.7	3.5	2.2	4.9	5.4	4.3
1983	31.4	2.9	2.6	5.4	5.0	5.9
1984	48.4	3.5	3.4	5.8	4.7	6.5
1985	45.0	3.2	3.1	4.6	5.6	4.6
1986	34.6	1.8	2.5	3.9	5.0	4.7
1987	38.9	2.4	2.4	3.6	4.0	7.8
1988	75.4	3.7	3.7	4.8	5.4	6.2
1989	63.3	3.4	3.2	4.2	5.0	7.2
1990	60.3	2.0	3.1	3.3	3.6	10.2
1991	66.0	2.6	2.9	4.8	5.1	14.5
1992	70.1	3.8	2.9	5.9	6.0	14.9
1993	66.0	2.6	3.0	5.7	6.3	16.3

1. Change in reserve money divided by GNP.
2. Consumer price inflation times the reserve money/GNP ratio.
3. Reserve money stock multiplied by "long-term" interest rate (one-year deposit rate until 1985, one-year bond rate thereafter).
4. Reserve money stock multiplied by three-month interest rate (deposit rate until 1985, Treasury bill rate thereafter).
Source: Central Bank of Turkey, *Quarterly Bulletin*, and OECD.

curve'' in public finance. Such a relationship allows in principle the estimation of the inflation rate at which the revenues from seigniorage would attain a maximum. This has been done by regressing (monetary) seigniorage on a quadratic function of the rate of inflation.[41] The estimation result suggests that a maximum level of seigniorage revenues would be attained at around 67 per cent consumer price inflation (Diagram 9). Although this estimate is not very robust, it is striking that the inflation rate has been rather stable over the past five years in the vicinity of this figure irrespective of the cyclical position of the economy, which would not be inconsistent with the need of fiscal authorities to extract as much seigniorage as possible.

Diagram 9. **SEIGNIORAGE AND INFLATION**

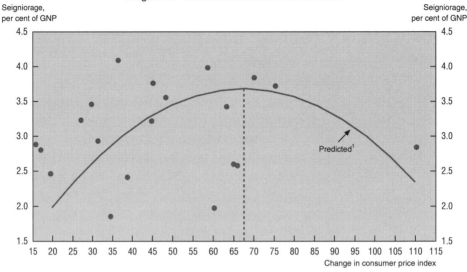

1. Predicted values from the regression shown in footnote 41.
Source: OECD.

How tight is the relationship between public-sector deficits and inflation?

Although it is widely accepted that high public-sector deficits financed by money creation inevitably lead to high inflation, the empirical relationship between these variables is often not very tight. However, in the case of Turkey it appears relatively straightforward to relate overall inflation as measured by the GNP deflator to the public-sector borrowing requirement, the degree of "monetisation" of the economy – expressed as the share of reserve money in GNP – and the supply of goods and services. Such a relationship has been successfully tested on an earlier occasion (see the 1990/91 OECD *Economic Survey of Turkey,* Chapter II) and retains its statistical significance over a larger sample period, although the goodness of fit seems to have deteriorated in recent years.[42] In spite of its simplicity, the estimated relationship explains nearly half of the variance in GNP inflation (Diagram 10). The model suggests that at the margin a cut in the PSBR/GNP ratio by 1 percentage point, accompanied by a

Diagram 10. **ACTUAL AND ESTIMATED CHANGES
IN THE GNP DEFLATOR**

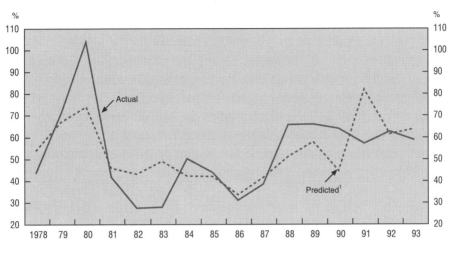

1. The model is presented in footnote 42.
Source: OECD.

commensurate reduction in monetary deficit financing and with everything else unchanged,[43] would lower overall inflation by some 15 percentage points.

New initiatives in structural reform

The comprehensive structural adjustment programme launched at the beginning of the 1980s had lost some of its momentum by the end of the decade. A law on the introduction of unemployment insurance, which could help to cope with the inevitable labour shedding in restructuring loss-making SEEs, is still subject to intra-governmental discussion. Recently implemented measures, such as the changes to the financial system – sketched out in the 1992/93 OECD *Economic Survey of Turkey,* chapter II – were more in the form of fine-tuning and harmonisation of existing rules than of sweeping reform.

The tax reform bill of early 1993 was withdrawn by the new government in the summer and a new proposal was submitted to the Parliament, which passed the tax reform law in December 1993. A major provision of the new law is the cut in the corporate tax rate from 46 to 25 per cent combined with the abolition of several tax exemptions which in the past had caused many firms to pay far less than 25 per cent. A floor of 20 per cent has been set for the minimum effective tax rate (after exemptions). Moreover, a 20 per cent withholding tax on taxable profits of family companies has been introduced in addition to the corporation tax. Taxpayers who currently pay income tax based on lump-sum assessments are offered a special cut in their tax liabilities by half during three years if they switch from the lump-sum system to the income declaration system. The latter measure is aimed at limiting under-declaration (or under-assessment) of company and self-employed earnings, a major cause of foregone tax revenues. It will help to shift the burden of income tax away from wage earners towards the self-employed, who account for more than one-half of total employment, a far higher proportion than in most other OECD countries.

Recent initiatives to implement a customs union with the European Community (EC), envisaged for 1995, may give a new and strong impetus to structural reform efforts. The "Ankara Agreement" of 1963, which created an "Association" between Turkey and the EEC, foresaw the establishment of a customs union in several steps. After a preparatory stage, detailed rules and terms for a transitional stage were laid out in the "Additional Protocol" of 23 December 1970. However, little progress was made during the "cooling-off" period in the 1970s and the 1980s. In 1988, Turkey declared a five-year timetable for tariff reductions; the latest cut was implemented at the beginning of 1993, when the average tariff rate for EC goods was reduced from 21.6 per cent to 15.2 per cent. On 8 November 1993, the EEC-Turkey Association Council reaffirmed the decision of both parties to achieve effective completion of the customs union in 1995. Subsequently, the average tariff rate was reduced further, by about 5 percentage points at the beginning of 1994.

The envisaged customs union is confined to industrial goods (*i.e.* for the time being, agricultural products are excluded from the agreement) and foresees the free circulation of these goods between the EC and Turkey. To this effect, duties as well as quantitative restrictions on imports are to be eliminated by 1995. This implies that the EC has to abolish its quota on textiles and apparels, which is of particular importance for Turkey, as these sectors account for 37 per cent of export earnings, some 14 per cent of GNP and more than a fifth of manufacturing employment. Negotiations of the special provisions applying to agricultural products, steel and coal are planned in 1994. The customs union also requires Turkey to adopt the European Community's common external tariff in its trade with third countries and to adhere to the common trade policy.

Another consequence of customs union is that the trade-related legislation and commercial law of Turkey have to be brought into closer convergence with that of the EC. This implies legal changes in the fields of competition policy, state aids, anti-dumping provisions, intellectual property rights, technical regulations concerning industrial products and public procurement, and further revisions to the laws on banking and insurance. In this vein, a variety of amendments to the Turkish banking law were implemented in the autumn of 1993, among them an increase in the minimum required capital for the establishment of banks. Furthermore, a draft law on competition policy, whose purpose is to prevent the abuse of dominant market positions and to prohibit cartel agreements, has been submitted to the relevant parliamentary commissions. The proposed bill declares unlawful mergers or acquisitions which risk strengthening a dominant position of an enterprise and/or significantly impeding competition in a certain market. Moreover, it is planned to establish a new institution which will ensure the compliance with competition legislation. A patent law bill has also been drafted, which takes into account findings from the examination of the respective regulations in Germany, Austria, Switzerland, Japan, Spain as well as the European Patent Convention. Work is in process on law bills dealing with copyright protection, consumer protection and trade arrangements in the fruit and vegetable markets.

Free access to large EC markets and the provision of cheaper imports of production inputs will give a boost to Turkish exports. The reduction of tariffs and import duties will enhance competition in domestic markets, thereby benefiting consumers and contributing to overall price stabilisation. It will also promote an acceleration of structural adjustment in industry. The loss of government revenues from import duties, including a levy on luxury goods earmarked for the Mass Housing Fund and estimated to be of the order of $3 billion a year, will add to budgetary strains; fiscal savings from the abolition of export incentives and higher excise tax rates could be a way to offset the revenue losses at least in part. Another potential risk is that a strong increase in imports – everything else unchanged – would add to the already large trade deficit.

Full implementation of the customs union will bring about substantial structural change accompanied by unavoidable adjustment cost, but altogether, an assessment of the benefits suggests that over time the adjustment cost will be more than compensated for by a large margin. Stronger competition from EC imports will encourage greater efficiencies in production and distribution and stimulate the adoption of new technologies. That part of foreign direct investment which has been motivated in the past by the protection of the domestic market is likely to be discouraged; but on the other hand, the customs union will create powerful new incentives for foreign investment in sectors where production in Turkey offers competitive advantages.

III. Agricultural policy

Introduction

Agriculture has economy-wide importance in Turkey. Nearly half of its population still live in rural areas, and internal migration towards urban areas continues at a fast pace. Agricultural policy has hence had significant regional policy dimensions and, perhaps partly because of this, has been an important exception to the overall policy orientation adopted since the early 1980s towards greater reliance on market forces. Policies of open-ended farm price support resulted in inefficient production and the level of government support approaching the OECD average. The State-owned enterprises in the agro-food sector are responsible for some 60 per cent of the borrowing requirement of the SEEs in 1993 even after large budgetary transfers from the central government. Agricultural policy has thus become one of the main culprits responsible for the unchecked deterioration in public finances.

Turkey appears to have enormous economic potential in a wide variety of agricultural products. It is, however, at a cross-roads concerning the strategy it will adopt in managing this potential. Price support measures taken over the last several years give rise to a number of questions and concerns about the future course of policy. Will Turkey – using an institutional apparatus left largely intact from the interventionist policies of the sixties and seventies – opt for the high protection levels common throughout much of the OECD area? Or, alternatively, will it adopt a market-oriented approach to agricultural and rural development, with the government promoting welfare through the development of social services and through appropriate investment in infrastructure and in agricultural research and extension, but leaving most other decisions to the market?

The socio-economics of Turkish agriculture

Agricultural policies in Turkey have developed against a background of rapid economic, demographic and social change. Although agriculture has become a less significant sector in the Turkish economy over a period of several decades, it still accounts for larger shares of total output (16 per cent in 1993) and employment (42 per cent) than in any other OECD country. These shares have tended to fall over time (Diagram 11). In many ways the transition that the Turkish economy is undergoing – with high economic growth and the release of agricultural labour to other sectors – resembles those experienced by many OECD countries during the 1950s and 1960s.

Population growth rates in Turkey, exceeding 2 per cent annually, have been well over three times the average rate for the OECD. The highest fertility rates are to be found in rural areas, with out-migration rates from these areas also

Diagram 11. **SHARE OF AGRICULTURE IN TOTAL EMPLOYMENT AND TOTAL OUTPUT**

Per cent

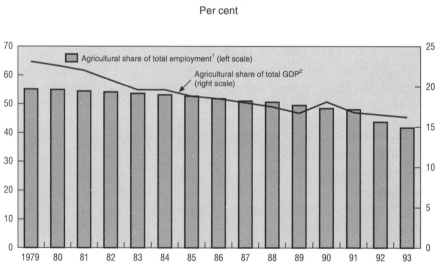

1. Data for 1979-87 are from *Developments Before 6th Five-Year Development Plan;* data for 1988-91 are from SPO *Annual Programmes;* data for 1992-93 are SPO estimates.
2. Data for 1991-92 are SIS estimates dated March 1991; data for 1993 are from the SIS *Annual Programme.*
Source: State Planning Organisation and State Institute of Statistics.

tending to be high. Although migration abroad has slowed considerably, internal migration – mainly from rural areas to industrial towns – continues at a rapid pace, driven largely by income differentials (Table 20). Out-migration does not affect all rural areas equally, however: many of the people moving to the large cities come from the rural provinces of eastern Anatolia, several of which lost more than 15 per cent of their populations between the 1985 and the 1990 censuses. On the whole, though, the degree of urbanisation appears to be about average or slightly below average for middle income developing economies.[44]

Experience in the OECD countries has shown that rural-urban migration is largely an inevitable consequence of industrialisation. There are nevertheless grounds for concern that this market-driven internal migration process may be reinforced by other regional disparities that are perhaps less essential to development. In particular, the data point to wide disparities in broader indicators of regional welfare. Table 21 shows two standard welfare indicators – infant mortality rates and educational attainment rates – for selected regions (Diagram 12). With regard to infant mortality, the overall average for Turkey (at 66 deaths per 1000 births) puts it well above those of other countries at similar levels of development.[45] The regional breakdown – which shows this figure rising as high as 114 in one province – suggests that there is room for improvement in the performance of the various government services charged with stemming these largely avoidable deaths.[46] The educational attainment figures paint a similar picture regarding education services in rural areas, with the illiteracy rate exceeding 35 per cent in East Anatolia, as compared with 12 per cent in the Marmara region. Although some of the remoter rural regions of Turkey undoubtedly represent a daunting challenge for social service providers and although some progress has been made,[47] these regional differences in social services may, by reinforcing the income gap, contribute to rural-urban migration.

Reflecting these income and social welfare considerations is the socio-economic stratification of the farm population. Turkey's agricultural workforce appears to be a varied one, with the sector exhibiting a diverse range of farm types. Turkish farms are usually operated by a farm family and sometimes employ hired workers. Although relatively few data are available on farm households, owner-operators of fully commercial farms (mainly in western Turkey) appear to exhibit human capital mixes that are similar to those of their counterparts elsewhere in the OECD area: comparatively low levels of formal education

Table 20. **Value-added per employee in the agricultural and non-agricultural sectors**

Years	Agriculture's share of value added	Agriculture's share of employment	Value added per agricultural worker as a percentage of value added per non-agricultural worker
1979	24	56	25
1980	36	55	47
1981	22	54	23
1982	20	54	22
1983	19	53	21
1984	19	52	22
1985	18	51	22
1986	18	50	23
1987	17	49	21
1988	16	46	22
1989	16	48	21
1990	17	48	23
1991	15	47	19
1992	14	44	21

Source: State Planning Organisation, *Economical and Social Indicators*, and State Institute of Statistics.

Table 21. **Welfare indicators by province or region**

Data are for mid- to late 1980s

	Provinces				Turkey
	Mus	Sanliurfa	Adiyaman	Sivas	
Infant mortality rate [1]	93	98	94	114	66 [3]

	Region				
	Marmara Aegean	Mediterranean	Black Sea	Central Anatolia	East Anatolia
Educational status of adults [2]					
Illiteracy rate	12.3	21.2	20.5	17.2	35.4
Graduates of primary school	52.7	52.2	51.0	51.8	40.2

1. Number of infants who die in their first year, per thousand.
2. Adults are defined as persons aged 12 and over.
3. According to World Bank figures, which use a slightly different statistical category, Turkey averaged 58 deaths per 1 000 live births in 1991. This compares with an average of 38 for middle income developing countries and 34 for upper-middle income developing countries. *World Bank Development Report*, 1993.
Source: Istanbul Chamber of Commerce, *A Social and Economic Atlas of Turkey*; demographic and educational attainment figures are those published in 1989 by the State Institute of Statistics.

Diagram 12. **MAP OF TURKEY**

Agricultural regions[1]

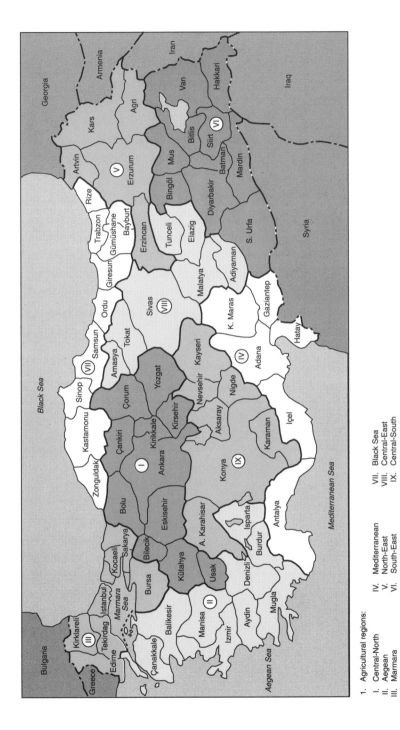

1. Agricultural regions:

I. Central-North   IV. Mediterranean   VII. Black Sea
II. Aegean   V. North-East   VIII. Central-East
III. Marmara   VI. South-East   IX. Central-South

Source: State Institute of Statistics.

are combined with high levels of sector-specific know-how and of general management skills.[48] For the vast majority of the farm workforce, however, – especially those operating on subsistence or mixed subsistence/commercial farms – educational attainment is very low, as are informally-acquired levels of agronomic and managerial skills. Located at the very bottom of the agricultural incomes and wealth hierarchy are the landless agricultural workers. These workers have negligible levels of physical and human capital and are among the most vulnerable members of rural society.

Census data (Table 22) show that the pattern of land ownership is very skewed – with 1990 census data revealing that 5.3 per cent of farm households own 37 per cent of the land, while 34.9 per cent of the households own only 5.6 per cent of the land. The census data also point to wide regional variations in the pattern of land ownership among farm households.[49] This variation reflects in part the differing natures of the crops grown in the different regions. It may also reflect regional differences in how farm households generate income (the relative

Table 22. **Number and average size of farm holdings in Turkey, 1980 and 1990**

Size of farm holdings (hectares)	Number	Per cent of total	Average size of farm holdings (hectares)	Per cent of total agricultural area
		1980		
0.1-1.9	1 010 649	28	0.9	4
2.0-4.9	1 164 742	33	3.1	16
5.0-9.9	738 376	21	6.6	21
10.0-19.9	412 523	12	12.9	23
20.0-49.9	194 186	5	27.7	24
50.0+	29 439	1	92.9	12
Total	3 558 815	100	6.4	100
		1990		
0.1-1.9	1 385 129	35	0.9	6
2.0-4.9	1 274 609	32	3.0	17
5.0-9.9	713 149	18	6.6	19
10.0-19.9	383 323	10	12.8	21
20.0-49.9	173 774	4	26.7	20
50.0+	36 838	10	109.0	17
Total	3 966 822	100	5.9	100

Source: State Institute of Statistics, *Agricultural Population Census, 1980 and 1990.*

extensive farming countries, but they are only around half the level of yields in Europe.[55] This reflects Turkey's relatively abundant land endowment[56] – which favours an extensive farming system – as well as the farming techniques and agro-climatic conditions prevailing in Turkey's regions.[57] A smaller portion of output growth has been due to increase in the area sown to field crops. Although there have been impressive increases in livestock yields, they remain low relative to other OECD countries, including those in the Mediterranean area.

Turkey's 78.1 million hectares of mostly rugged land area is exposed to both maritime and continental weather patterns. This, combined with a varied topography, produces several distinct climatic zones allowing a wide range of crops to be produced (Table 25). Climate and geography also have an important bearing on the location and type of animal husbandry carried out in Turkey. Intensive animal husbandry is carried out in the regions of Western Anatolia and Thrace – *i.e.* near the major ports and population centres. Milk is produced throughout the country, although the largest dairies are concentrated in the west.

Table 25. **Regional agricultural output patterns**

Regions	Principal products	Average temperature in °C	Days with humidity	Days with snow
Central-North	Cereals, rice, vegetables, pulses, fruits	11	60	22
Agean	Olives, grapes, cotton, tobacco, pulses, vegetables, tubers	16	65	0
Marmara	Sunflower, rice, roots, sugarbeets	14	70	10
Mediterranean	Cotton, cereals, citrus, rice, vegetables, pulses	18	62	0
North-East	Fodder, wheat, tubers, pulses, livestock	7	60	100
South-East	Fodder, cereals, tubers, pulses, vegetables, grapes, livestock, pistachio, fruits	9	50	1-80
Black Sea	Hazelnuts, tea, rice, tobacco	14	75	10
Central-East	Fodder, cereals, fruits, tobacco, sugarbeets	12	55	30
Central-South	Cereals, sugarbeets, grapes, pulses, vegetables, tubes, livestock	11	60	22

Source: Data provided by the Turkish authorities.

Water and agriculture

Water is a major limiting factor for agriculture over much of Turkey. While average annual precipitation is highest in the Black Sea Region (1120 mm), and exceeds 800 mm/year in some of the other coastal areas, the remaining 70 per cent of the country averages less the 500 mm a year. In the highland plains of Central Anatolia it averages less than 400 mm. This is roughly similar to the rainfall pattern of the States of Queensland and New South Wales in Australia.

All water rights, with minor exceptions, are vested in the State. This principle, however, allows private withdrawal of ground and surface water by riparian owners (OECD 1992, page 59). No fee is charged to farmers for the resource value of the water they use for irrigation (underpricing of water used for irrigation purposes is common in the arid zones of the OECD), although farmers who grow crops sown on irrigated land do contribute towards part of the costs of operating, maintaining and investing in irrigation infrastructure.

Irrigation projects – some of very large magnitude – are gradually helping to overcome this natural limitation. In 1993, the total irrigated area covered by the two main institutions responsible for installing and operating the public irrigation works[58] is estimated to have reached more than 3.2 million hectares, which represents a 3.5 per cent annual growth rate since 1970. If irrigation works built by farmers themselves are included, the total irrigated area was probably around 4.1 million hectares, or 15 per cent of the arable land surface. The scope for further expansion appears to be considerable.

Large-scale public projects include the huge combined hydroelectric and irrigation scheme, the South-East Anatolia project (GAP). The recently completed Atatürk Dam (commanding 882 000 gross hectares of irrigable land) is part of this project, which is entirely located in one of Turkey's poorer regions. When complete, the GAP will include 22 dams and 19 hydro-electric power plants and could potentially irrigate some 1.7 million hectares; less than 4 per cent of the target irrigated area had been developed as of 1993.[59]

A recent World Bank report (1993) notes that the successful development and management of irrigation infrastructure is key to the future development of Turkish agriculture. Average value added per irrigated hectare in Turkey is 2.6 times that of a rain-fed hectare. In crops that are very sensitive to the availability of irrigation (for example, green vegetables, fruits and nuts, nonindustrial tomatoes), net incomes under irrigation are frequently fifteen times the incomes for rain-fed agriculture and sometimes as much as 50 times rain-fed levels. In 1990, the irrigated area – estimated to comprise 17 per cent of the land under crops – contributed 34 per cent of the GDP derived from all crops (rain-fed plus irrigated).

Irrigation projects – because of their income-generating effects and because irrigated crops tend to be labour intensive – also appear to contribute to retaining people in rural areas. The World Bank report concludes that irrigated agriculture has helped to slow the pace of rural out-migration in Turkey: in a sample of 880 villages located in 21 public irrigation schemes in 19 provinces, village populations continued to increase in absolute terms from 1985 to 1990, whereas the surrounding villages and rural Turkey as a whole registered absolute population declines over the same period. The study concludes that irrigation has contributed "substantially" to a deceleration of the rate at which workers leave their villages in pursuit of non-agricultural jobs in urban areas. Thus, properly-targeted irrigation projects could contribute importantly to the incomes and stability of many rural regions.

Looked at as a whole, progress made to date in irrigation – although considerable – has been bought at a very high public cost. This appears to be largely due to inter-related deficiencies in pricing and project governance which have, in turn, led to poor project selection and to management problems for schemes once they have been completed. With regard to project selection, it would appear that the mix of public investment has not focused primarily on those projects yielding the highest rates of return. Evidence of this can be seen most readily in the low "irrigation ratios" – the ratio between actual and potential irrigated land – that characterise many of these schemes. The results of a 1990 study[60] covering 189 irrigation schemes and 1.24 million equipped hectares with an aggregate irrigation ratio of 64 per cent showed that the most common reason cited for not irrigating when irrigation services became available was that good agro-climatic conditions made it unnecessary.[61] This suggests that irrigation schemes have been installed in areas where low returns on investment are to be expected. In addition, the timing of the projects has posed problems. Often too many projects were initiated simultaneously relative to available investment funds, causing completion times to be unduly drawn out. Organisation and management of some public irrigation schemes, once they have been built, also appear to be beset by serious problems.[62]

Comparative advantage in agriculture

Although relatively little is known about the commercial potential of agriculture in some of Turkey's remoter regions, the general outlook for much of the sector appears to be quite promising. Estimates of domestic resource costs in the crops sector, for example, would seem to point to significant comparative advantage in a very wide range of products.[63] Turkey's proximity to Europe, the Middle East and North Africa give it easy access to large markets through the Black Sea to the north, the Aegean Sea to the west and the Mediterranean to the south. Likewise, its internal market – characterised by high population growth rates and growing incomes – should also experience rapid growth in demand for more food of higher quality.

Thus, agriculture in Turkey appears to hold the promise of making a major contribution to Turkey's economic development. The exact extent of agriculture's ultimate contribution will depend on several factors. First, policy developments within Turkey – including whether or not the government is successful in streamlining subsidies and in privatising and deregulating the agrifood sector – will determine the degree to which the sector's commercial and technical capabilities will improve. Second, the success of trade liberalisation efforts – both in multilateral fora and in neighbouring regions – will determine the size of the markets available to Turkey. Third, the attainment of political stability in the adjacent regions (especially in the former Soviet states) could create new outlets (and possibly new competitors) for Turkey's production.

Agricultural support policies

Objectives and historical developments

The objectives of agricultural policy, as set out in successive Five Year Development Plans, are to stabilise agricultural prices; to provide adequate and stable incomes for those working in agriculture; to meet the nutritional needs of a growing population; to increase yields and outputs; to reduce the vulnerability of production to weather conditions; to develop rural areas; to develop the export potential of agriculture and to promote the application of modern agricultural techniques.

Over the last several decades, the government has implemented a variety of measures in pursuit of these objectives. In the crops sector, domestic price supports extended by means of intervention purchases have been bolstered with quantitative import controls and tariffs (changes made over the last decade have replaced some quantitative controls with tariffs). In the livestock sector, border measures have been the main mechanism used to support prices. In addition to these price supports, the government attempts to support farm incomes through a variety of input subsidies, supplemented at times with rather small direct payments to farmers.

Taken together, these measures have given rise to a certain volume of "transfers",[64] financed either by taxpayers or by consumers. The Secretariat has estimated the value of such transfers over the 1979 to 1993 period.[65] These estimates – called the producer subsidy equivalent (PSE)[66] – show that the level of support (measured as a percentage of the value of production) has tended to increase in recent years, although there have been wide year-to-year variations.

The provisional PSE estimates for individual crops and for various aggregates – crops, livestock and total – are presented in Table 26. During the period for which calculations are available (1979-93), total support (as measured by the percentage PSE) was lower than the OECD average percentage PSE. However, in the three year period 1991-93, total support is estimated to have risen to around 40 per cent, double the rate of the 1979-81 period and close to the OECD average. Thus, at a very aggregate level, the thrust of Turkish agricultural policy over the last several years has been to raise support levels significantly.[67]

As shown in Diagram 13, the most important PSE component in recent years has been market price support, which currently accounts for more than four-fifths of the total. However, market price support was small – and sometimes negative – during the early to mid-1980s when, in effect, Turkey's agricultural trade policy taxed exports and subsidised imports. Subsidies designed to reduce input costs – including concessional credits, fertiliser subsidies and payments for operation and maintenance of irrigation structures and equipment[68] – tend to be quite an important PSE component for Turkey.

75

Table 26. **Producer subsidy equivalents**

	Units	1979-86 (average)	1987	1988	1989	1990	1991	1992 Estimate	1993 Provisional
Turkey									
Wheat									
Gross total PSE	TL mn	29 214	650 658	1 477 640	1 886 718	2 185 169	6 944 776	5 701 006	9 042 540
Gross unit PSE	TL/t	2 115	42 502	88 010	142 203	131 955	411 148	356 750	532 729
Gross percentage PSE	%	1	44	52	42	26	54	30	27
Producer NAC[1]		1.06	1.60	1.86	1.58	1.31	1.93	1.37	1.32
Coarse Grains									
Gross total PSE	TL mn	31 664	299 871	145 646	371 142	1 323 413	2 026 061	3 738 699	7 276 432
Gross unit PSE	TL/t	4 717	35 917	16 916	57 723	153 208	265 406	448 438	855 296
Gross percentage PSE	%	15	44	11	20	38	46	42	51
Producer NAC[1]		1.16	1.66	1.11	1.22	1.55	1.72	1.65	1.90
Oilseeds									
Gross total PSE	TL mn	17 714	134 275	96 130	325 116	385 436	648 548	1 166 672	1 669 779
Gross unit PSE	TL/t	25 067	122 068	83 591	260 573	448 180	810 685	1 230 163	1 703 856
Gross percentage PSE	%	29	57	23	39	52	54	47	43
Producer NAC[1]		1.36	2.00	1.25	1.56	1.86	1.95	1.77	1.65
Sugar (Refined equivalent)									
Gross total PSE	TL mn	22 719	77 093	107 941	96 298	434 331	1 424 524	2 706 245	3 539 413
Gross unit PSE	TL/t	16 991	46 980	82 958	70 339	242 779	754 515	1 386 283	1 769 707
Gross percentage PSE	%	29	28	23	11	23	44	50	43
Producer NAC[1]		1.32	1.32	1.24	1.10	1.27	1.69	1.85	1.66
Milk									
Net total PSE	TL mn	107 853	247 870	344 751	615 035	2 306 634	3 438 029	6 683 525	9 388 009
Net unit PSE	TL/t	23 417	47 973	62 867	114 768	439 426	610 803	1 150 091	1 564 668
Net percentage PSE	%	47	35	25	27	58	53	54	50
Producer NAC[1]		1.84	1.52	1.30	1.35	2.37	2.15	2.19	2.04
Beef and Veal									
Net total PSE	TL mn	20 240	(893)	73 977	212 947	681 975	1 956 648	4 078 503	7 226 242
Net unit PSE	TL/t	66 246	(2 389)	190 766	599 629	1 872 629	4 721 642	9 839 573	16 927 927
Net percentage PSE	%	14	(0)	7	13	24	35	41	44
Producer NAC[1]		1.16	1.00	1.07	1.15	1.33	1.56	1.72	1.83

Sheepmeat									
Net total PSE	TL mn	15 318	132 161	98 312	320 641	517 008	979 305	1 534 655	2 382 228
Net unit PSE	TL/t	52 510	476 470	282 347	933 166	1 626 321	3 007 694	5 161 974	7 940 760
Net percentage PSE	%	9	22	10	20	21	20	20	19
Producer NAC[1]		1.10	1.28	1.10	1.24	1.26	1.25	1.24	1.23
Crops									
Gross total PSE	TL mn	101 344	1 161 898	1 827 357	2 650 374	4 326 348	11 643 908	13 315 124	21 528 163
Gross percentage PSE	%	12	43	36	34	30	50	37	36
Producer NAC[1]		1.12	1.62	1.47	1.42	1.37	1.84	1.51	1.49
Livestock products									
Net total PSE	TL mn	167 860	412 418	745 178	1 539 407	4 024 617	6 378 209	14 307 529	23 084 727
Net percentage PSE	%	26	17	17	22	34	31	38	37
Producer NAC[1]		1.33	1.20	1.19	1.27	1.54	1.47	1.63	1.64
All products									
Net total PSE	TL mn	269 204	1 574 316	2 572 535	4 189 781	8 352 965	18 022 117	27 622 652	44 612 871
Net percentage PSE	%	18	30	27	28	32	41	38	37
Producer NAC[1]		1.20	1.40	1.33	1.35	1.42	1.66	1.57	1.55
Net total PSE	**US$ mn**	**991**	**1 841**	**1 813**	**1 976**	**3 204**	**4 323**	**4 025**	**4 067**
Comparative indicators									
Australia									
Net total PSE	US$ mn	1 003	1 014	989	988	1 317	1 264	1 116	992
Net percentage PSE	%	10	10	8	7	12	12	10	10
EC[2]									
Net total PSE	US$ mn	39 552	71 634	69 093	59 505	82 442	83 611	84 928	76 984
Net percentage PSE	%	37	49	46	40	47	48	48	47
United States									
Net total PSE	US$ mn	22 790	35 327	26 286	23 145	27 328	23 938	25 272	27 882
Net percentage PSE	%	21	32	24	20	22	21	20	22
OECD									
Net total PSE	US$ mn	98 082	164 526	153 814	136 620	167 416	165 460	170 011	162 321
Net percentage PSE	%	33	46	42	37	41	42	42	42

1. The producer nominal assistance coefficient (NAC) is defined as the producer price and unit PSE divided by world reference price (adjusted for transportation costs).
2. EC: EC-10 for 1979-85, EC-12 from 1986; includes ex-GDR since 1990.
Source: OECD.

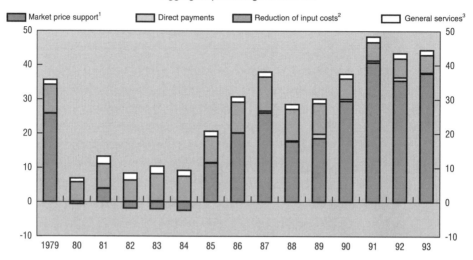

Diagram 13. **STRUCTURE OF AGRICULTURAL SUPPORT**
Aggregate percentage of net PSE

1. Net of feed adjustment.
2. Includes capital grants, interest concessions, fertilizer subsidies, cultivation services, seed and breeding improvements, pesticides, and irrigation operation and maintenance.
3. Includes research, advisory, training; inspection; pest and disease control; and marketing and promotion.
Source : OECD.

The trends in the percentage consumer subsidy equivalent (CSE)[69] in Turkey have largely mirrored those of the PSE, indicating that consumers have paid most of the bill for rising agricultural support (see Table 27). Over the latest three years, policies have imposed an average implicit tax on consumers of around 35 per cent, a tripling of Turkey's average implicit tax rate since the period 1979-81. Again, in recent years, this implicit tax rate has risen to levels that bring it close to the OECD average. Schematically described, Turkish policy seems to be evolving toward a support system in which the bulk of the subsidies take the form of market price support financed by a food consumption tax. This would appear to be incompatible with the government's objective of improving the quality of the diet of the Turkish population.

The remainder of this section reviews the implementation of agricultural policy and identifies some problems associated with the current institutional set-

Table 27. **Consumer subsidy equivalents**

	Units	1979-86 (average)	1987	1988	1989	1990	1991	1992 Estimate	1993 Provisional
Turkey									
Crops									
Total CSE	TL mn	20 417	(749 624)	(1 108 439)	(1 618 835)	(2 800 390)	(8 788 902)	(9 038 121)	(14 671 219)
Percentage CSE	%	2	(28)	(22)	(17)	(17)	(39)	(20)	(25)
Consumer NAC[1]		0.98	1.39	1.29	1.21	1.24	1.65	1.33	1.28
Livestock products									
Total CSE	TL mn	(142 326)	(356 771)	(371 840)	(1 149 239)	(4 255 345)	(7 352 768)	(15 914 511)	(26 774 656)
Percentage CSE	%	(22)	(14)	(9)	(17)	(35)	(34)	(40)	(41)
Consumer NAC[1]		1.29	1.17	1.09	1.20	1.54	1.65	1.66	1.70
All products									
Total CSE	TL mn	(121 909)	(1 106 395)	(1 480 279)	(2 768 075)	(7 055 735)	(16 141 671)	(24 952 632)	(41 445 875)
Percentage CSE	%	(8)	(21)	(16)	(17)	(27)	(37)	(33)	(33)
Consumer NAC[1]		1.09	1.27	1.19	1.21	1.36	1.59	1.49	1.50
Total CSE	US$ mn	**(412)**	**(1 294)**	**(1 043)**	**(1 306)**	**(2 706)**	**(3 872)**	**(3 637)**	**(3 779)**
Comparative indicators									
Australia									
Total CSE	US$ mn	(227)	(291)	(280)	(296)	(378)	(388)	(357)	(300)
Percentage CSE	%	(6)	(8)	(6)	(6)	(9)	(9)	(8)	(7)
EC[2]									
Total CSE	ECU mn	(29 874)	(53 400)	(47 676)	(42 865)	(49 545)	(52 332)	(48 770)	(44 055)
Total CSE	US$ mn	(30 391)	(61 620)	(56 342)	(47 197)	(62 900)	(64 687)	(63 122)	(52 080)
Percentage CSE	%	(30)	(46)	(40)	(34)	(40)	(42)	(39)	(35)
United States									
Total CSE	US$ mn	(10 051)	(13 410)	(8 051)	(8 587)	(12 927)	(10 903)	(11 031)	(11 518)
Total CSE	ECU mn	(10 416)	(11 621)	(6 813)	(7 799)	(10 182)	(8 821)	(8 523)	(9 743)
Percentage CSE	%	(11)	(15)	(8)	(9)	(12)	(11)	(11)	(11)
OECD									
Total CSE	US$ mn	(66 197)	(125 392)	(117 704)	(103 029)	(124 025)	(126 289)	(126 334)	(119 767)
Total CSE	ECU mn	(66 675)	(108 665)	(99 602)	(93 571)	(97 692)	(102 168)	(97 610)	(101 311)
Percentage CSE	%	(26)	(39)	(34)	(30)	(34)	(35)	(34)	(33)

1. The consumer nominal assistance coefficient (NAC) is defined as the domestic consumer price adjusted for consumer subsidies divided by world reference price (adjusted for transportation costs).
2. EC: 1979-85: EC-10 and 1986-90: EC-12; includes Ex-GDR since 1990.
Source: OECD.

79

up. In so doing, it first describes the institutions responsible for executing these policies. It then reviews the specific mechanisms of agricultural support. These are market price support (with particular emphasis on the system of intervention purchases), the related settings of agricultural trade policy and, finally, subsidies to inputs and for general services.

The implementation of agricultural policy

The implementation of agricultural policies in Turkey involves a large number of organisations. These include the State economic enterprises (SEEs), Agricultural Sales Co-operative Unions[70] (ASCUs), agricultural credit co-operatives, State-owned banks and other agencies with separate budgets (*e.g.* for rural development or for public works). The heavy involvement of SEEs in the execution of agricultural policies is the most visible legacy of the import substitution policies pursued during much of the post-war period. Indeed, a large share of the recent losses in the SEE sector are linked to intervention purchases and exports made in the context of growing subsidies. These institutions play an important role in some agri-food sectors. The SEE statutes define their responsibilities providing price support through commodity purchasing and stockpiling, disbursing subsidies, procuring and supplying inputs to farmers, pursuing regional development objectives, developing infrastructure and importing and exporting agricultural commodities. The Box (see below) lists the principal agricultural SEEs and describes the roles they play in their respective markets.

The government has begun the process of privatising some of its agricultural SEEs (those responsible for milk, meat and feed). But the firms at the top of the privatisation list are comparatively small, accounting in all cases for less than one-quarter of the shares of marketed output in their sectors. For the time being, the largest and most influential SEEs – the TMO (mainly grains), TSFAS (sugarbeet), TEKEL (tobacco) and ÇAYKUR (tea) – will remain in public hands. Taken together, these four enterprises dominate the markets for 25 per cent of Turkey's agricultural output and employ over 90 000 workers. Reluctance to move ahead on major privatisations in the agri-food sector reflects several considerations. First, privatisation would involve significant shedding of excess labour. Second, it is difficult to estimate the commercial value of the SEEs[71] under prevailing market and regulatory conditions and given their current policy

State economic enterprises in the agri-food sector

TMO – the Turkish Grain Board (also known as the Soil Products Office)

TMO is estimated to have run a TL 5 trillion deficit in 1993, or about 10 per cent of the total SEE deficit. TMO was established in 1938 to effect support purchases for wheat, coarse grains and other commodities. As defined in Article 4 of its statutes, its main functions are "to prevent a decrease in prices of domestic cereals below the normal level for producers and/or an abnormal increase in prices to the detriment of consumers, to take measures to organise the marketing of those commodities, where necessary to carry out duties involving pulses and oilseeds in addition to cereals in accordance with a government decision, and to operate the State monopoly on opium and narcotics." TMO controls the bulk of the nation's grain storage capacity and employs 7 650 people.

TSFAS – Turkish Sugar Factories Incorporated

TSFAS' deficit for 1993 is estimated at TL 4.4 trillion or 8 per cent of the total SEE deficit. With annual sales of over $1 billion and nearly 26 000 employees, TSFAS is currently Turkey's fifth-largest corporation and its third largest employer. In addition to maintaining its own staff, TSFAS contracts with nearly half a million sugarbeet growers. Up to 1984, TSFAS enjoyed a legal monopoly over production and until 1990 a monopoly in foreign trade of sugar. All but five of the 27 sugar plants currently operating in Turkey are fully owned by the company. Its statutes charge TSFAS with determining production (through forward contracts with growers), sales, investment and export and import policies as well as setting the prices of by-products within the framework of the 5-year development plans and the annual programmes.

TEKEL – the Directorate General for Tobacco and Tobacco Products, Salt and Alcohol Industry

TEKEL is estimated to have run a TL 13 trillion deficit in 1993, or about 24 per cent of the total SEE deficit. With annual sales of over $2 billion, TEKEL is Turkey's third largest company and its second largest employer, with some 50 000 employees. Until the Tobacco Law was amended in May 1986, TEKEL was the sole manufacturer of cigarettes and the only company allowed to import tobacco into Turkey. TEKEL is legally obliged to buy all tobacco not sold to private buyers and to stockpile what it cannot sell. Of the tobacco grown in 1991 and purchased in 1992, 36 per cent was purchased by the private sector and the remainder was purchased by TEKEL – 21 per cent for use in its own cigarette factories and the rest for support purposes. The functions of the TEKEL, as defined by its statutes, include "supporting producers, carrying out various activities and, where necessary, advancing funds with a view to increasing commodity quality and yield".

(continued on next page)

(continued)

CAYKUR – Tea Industry Corporation

CAYKUR was established in 1971. It currently operates 45 plants. In 1984 a law was passed abolishing its monopoly on tea purchases from growers and its monopoly of tea processing and sales. Private companies currently purchase around 20 per cent of Turkey's total output. However, the government still requires tea growers to obtain a cultivation permit from CAYKUR.

SEK – Turkish Milk Industry Corporation

SEK was created in 1963. In 1992, it was included in the list of enterprises slated for privatisation and in 1993 it was converted into a joint stock company. SEK carries out all types of commercial and financial activities related to the dairy industry: collecting milk, operating dairies and laboratories, sales and distribution. The SEK currently processes 5 per cent of the milk produced in Turkey in its 34 plants. With such a small market share the SEK can affect the market price only in a limited number of regional markets.

EBK – the Meat and Fish Organisation

EBK was set up in 1952. Its commercial activities include the purchasing of animals for slaughter, processing and marketing. The Organisation was slated for privatisation in 1992. Although EBK is the largest single purchaser of livestock in Turkey, it normally accounts for only 10 per cent or so of total domestic purchases. The only occasion when it was instructed to engage in support purchases was during the 1989 drought, when it bought up livestock threatened by a severe drought.

TZDK – Turkish Agricultural Supply Corporation

TZDK was established in 1943 and became a state economic enterprise in 1944. Under the provision of a 1973 decree, it was charged with the procurement and distribution of all inputs into the production of crops, including fertilisers. Between 1973 and 1986, when fertiliser imports by other operatives were permitted, it was essentially the sole buyer and wholesale distributor of fertilisers produced for domestic purposes. TZDK's share of the domestic market has since decline to around 10 per cent.

YEM SAN – Feed Industry Corporation

YEM SAN was established in 1956 to produce and market compound feed. The Corporation currently operates 26 plants with an annual capacity of 700 000 tonnes and controls a 10 per cent share of national feed industry production. It was designated for privatisation in 1992 and half of its factories had been sold by the end of 1992.

responsibilities. This is because much depends on how deregulation in the agri-food sector proceeds. Thus, privatisation, if it is to be successful, must go hand-in-hand with clarifying the rules for competition in their markets and, in a closely related matter, altering their roles in the execution of agricultural policy.

Because of these institutional arrangements, it is far from clear what portion of the total transfers engendered by price supports actually accrues to farmers. For the OECD area as a whole, this "transfer efficiency" tends in any case to be extremely low: Secretariat estimates show that, on average in the late 1980s, for three dollars of taxpayer or consumer outlay on market price support at most only one dollar reached farmers in the form of additional income.[72] The reasons behind this are numerous, but leakage of transfers to input-suppliers and to other vertically-related firms is key among them. Because of the prevalence of upstream and downstream players exercising significant market power relative to farmers, the Turkish agri-food sector might be expected to give rise to above average levels of "leakage".

Market price support

Table 28 lists the products that have been the object of intervention purchases since 1971.[73] One of the notable policy developments between 1980 and 1990 was the reduction in the number of commodities for which support purchases were made. This trend was reversed in 1991 and by 1992 support purchases had been extended to 26 commodities (from 10 in 1990). However, only six of these commodities – sugarbeet, tobacco, tea,[74] wheat, sunflower seeds and cotton – accounted for 90 per cent of support purchases in 1992.

As noted earlier, the institutions responsible for administering price supports are State economic enterprises and ASCUs. These organisations are a legacy of a decades-old system for administering prices (mainly in the crops sector) for the purpose of raising and stabilising producer incomes. Through time, however, policy-makers have enlarged the range of objectives that they pursue through market intervention, adding, in particular, the rural development and self-sufficiency objectives. As these were added, the difficulties involved in trying to balance competing objectives grew.

The government's task is made particularly difficult by the unpredictability of the factors it considers in determining support prices: the effects of weather; developments in foreign markets; consumer demand; stock changes; and, above

Table 28. **Agricultural commodity price supports**

	1979	1980	1981	1982	1983	1984	1985	1986	1987	1988	1989	1990	1991	1992
Wheat	x	x	x	x	x	x	x	x	x	x	x	x	x	x
Barley	x	x	x	x	x	x	x	x	x	x	x	x	x	x
Rye	x	x	x	x	x	x	x	x	x	x	x	x	x	x
Maize								x	x	x	x	x	x	x
Oats										x	x	x	x	x
Cotton	x	x	x	x	x	x	x	x	x				x	x
Tobacco	x	x	x	x	x	x	x	x	x	x	x	x	x	x
Tea	x	x	x	x	x	x								
Sugar beet	x	x	x	x	x	x	x	x	x	x	x	x	x	x
Sunflower seeds	x	x	x	x	x	x	x	x	x		x		x	x
Hazelnuts	x	x	x	x	x	x	x	x	x		x		x	x
Peanuts	x	x	x	x	x								x	x
Dried figs	x	x	x	x	x	x	x	x	x				x	x
Raisins (seedless)	x	x	x	x	x	x	x	x	x				x	x
Raisins	x	x		x				x						
Olive oil		x		x				x					x	x
Mohair	x	x	x	x		x			x	x	x	x	x	x
Merinos wool	x	x	x	x	x	x								
Silk cocoon	x	x										x	x	x
Pistachio nuts	x	x					x		x				x	x
Soya beans			x	x	x	x	x	x	x				x	x
Rape seed		x	x	x										
Rose for oil	x	x												x
Opium seed	x	x	x	x	x	x	x	x		x	x	x	x	x
Livestock	x										x			
Red lentils	x	x			x									x
Rape seed (kanola)										x				
Paddy														
Green lentils													x	x
Chickpeas					x								x	x
Red pepper													x	x
Olive													x	x

x = supported commodity.
Source: State Planning Organisation, *Annual Programmes.*

all, the rate of inflation – which has varied between 25 per cent and 100 per cent since the late 1970s, and which itself depends in part on decisions affecting agricultural prices.

The inevitable result of attempting to manage market outcomes *via* price supports and intervention purchases is that economic distortions are created and market balance is rarely if ever achieved: often too much is produced and output must be either stockpiled (thus, for example, Turkey has recently accumulated a "tobacco mountain")[75] or disposed of through subsidised sales on foreign markets. Alternatively, it sometimes happens that not enough is produced and importers must resort to purchasing large volumes at relatively short notice from foreign sources. The uncertainty confronting market participants is aggravated at times by delays in the publication of the official decrees announcing the support prices – these prices are generally not announced until well after the planting date and occasionally even after the delivery date. Thus, although the system may reduce market risk for some participants, it does so at a cost of far higher policy-induced uncertainty. Furthermore, the mixed signals created by these "managed" markets distort producer behaviour and inhibit the orderly development of private channels for managing price risk.

An important feature of the price support system is its *structure*: in Turkey, support prices are only in some cases differentiated by quality, rarely by location, and never by volume of sale. Despite the existence of formal limits on the acreage planted for a few commodities,[76] the purchases are effectively open-ended. These aspects of the price structure have been important in determining the level, mix and location of production. The lack of differentiation by quality in the price paid for commodities such as tea has encouraged growers to use inappropriate harvesting practices, has frustrated the industry's attempts to improve the quality of its end product, and has produced surpluses in excess of commercial demand. Even for commodities for which quality-differentiated prices exist, the number of product categories is still generally fewer than would exist if prices were determined in free markets. The application of a uniform price across the country for most commodities (tobacco and cotton, for which some regional price variation exists, are exceptions), with no accounting for transport cost differentials, has led to an inefficient geographic pattern of production. As a result, production has been relatively over-stimulated in regions remote from demand centres.

Support purchases are financed in a variety of ways. TMO receives automatic seasonal credits for its operations in grains and some pulses. These come from the Turkish Agricultural Bank and from the Central Bank. SEEs and ASCUs involved in support purchases for other commodities are subject to rather different financial treatment. Purchases are initially financed by the SEEs or the ASCUs; losses on such purchases are later compensated by the government. Due to these organisations' cash flow problems there are often delays in payments to farmers.

The system for financing support purchasing activities by SEEs and ASCUs has imposed large costs on the budget and, ultimately, taxpayers. As is pointed out in the Box, TMO, TEKEL and TSFAS are estimated to have accounted for 42 per cent of the total SEE deficit in 1993. Weak budgetary constraints on agricultural SEEs and ASCUs have allowed them to continue in business despite poor financial discipline and performance. Similarly, soft-budget constraints have enabled SEEs to finance stock-building through debt (including foreign credits), requiring in some years large debt write-offs by the government.

Problems with the Turkish price support system – highly variable support prices and levels of support, administered prices that are announced only after key production decisions have been made, and delays in payments by intervention agencies – attest to the difficulties inherent in trying to administer outcomes in a dynamic and complex market. Even overall demand-supply balance cannot be achieved, let alone equilibrium in the very complex intertemporal, spatial and quality dimensions. Recently the Turkish government – following a path already taken by many other OECD governments – has tried to replicate the market by introducing more frequent price adjustments and by establishing more quality-differentiated prices. Experiences of other OECD governments have shown that these attempts inevitably lead to an escalation of the administrative complexity of the agricultural programmes; they do not succeed in duplicating the pricing flexibility of freely functioning commodities markets.

Agricultural trade policies

Since its initial reform effort in the early 1980s, Turkey has made significant strides in opening up its borders to imports and reducing controls on exports. While self-sufficiency objectives have been pursued for some products,[77] the new policy regime has allowed imports of both processed and raw agricultural commodities to rise significantly (see Diagram 14). The general thrust of agricultural trade policy reform has been to replace quantitative trade constraint with a system of tariffs and duties.

The state trading monopolies, quotas, and other restrictions on agricultural imports and exports (along with most taxes on exports) that characterised Turkey's trade regime in the early 1980s[78] were gradually phased out and

Diagram 14. **TRENDS IN AGRICULTURAL TRADE**[1]

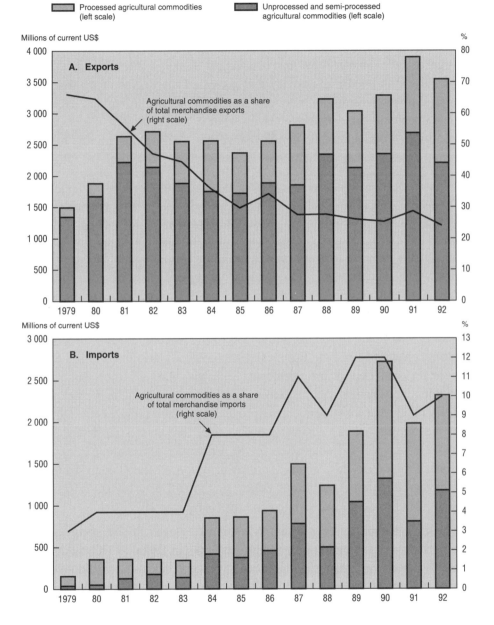

Processed agricultural commodities (left scale)

Unprocessed and semi-processed agricultural commodities (left scale)

Millions of current US$

A. Exports

Agricultural commodities as a share of total merchandise exports (right scale)

Millions of current US$

B. Imports

Agricultural commodities as a share of total merchandise imports (right scale)

1. Includes fish and forest products.
Source : Undersecretariat of Treasury and Foreign Trade, *Foreign Trade Statistics.*

replaced by tariffs and specific taxes on imports. In addition, various surcharges were consolidated, leaving just two kinds of tax on imports: customs duties (for which special concessional rates apply on some items imported from EC and EFTA Member countries) and "Mass Housing Fund payments" (effectively a surcharge to help finance low-cost housing in Turkey). All else equal, these changes have improved transparency and increased the degree of market information and price transmission between domestic and world markets. However, the government still subjects foreign trade in some commodities to administrative controls through non-automatic permit procedures. As of the beginning of 1993, the commodities subject to such controls were wheat, barley, maize, vegetable oil, sugar and certain dairy products.

As regards the level of protection accorded to agriculture by border measures, however, progress in very recent years has been mixed. Rates of border protection have been reduced for soybeans, for agricultural products that are used as inputs by the garment industry (particularly raw cotton, animal hides and skins and raw wool), and for agricultural inputs in general (hybrid seeds, breeding animals and chemical fertilisers). On the other hand, rates of border protection for wheat, sugar, poultry meat and eggs have been raised.

Turkey has made moves to harmonise its trade policies with those of the European Community and the European Free Trade Association and has entered into new regional trading arrangements. Still, the Mass Housing Fund levies remain important barriers to achievement of a customs union with the EC. In any case, it is likely that most agricultural products will be exempted initially from the full customs union, and separate provisions are foreseen for reciprocal preferential market access and adaptation to the Common Agricultural Policy. The Additional Protocol to the Ankara Agreement proposed that Turkey adopt elements of the Common Agricultural Policy by the end of a transition period of 22 years. This Protocol entered into force in November 1973.[79]

The government has been trying to encourage greater private-sector participation in trade. It has recently given the Turkish Grain Board (TMO) permission to lease its importing and storage facilities to private traders, for example. Yet it still exempts the TMO from paying the Mass Housing Fund levy on imported wheat, barley and maize, allowing the company to earn extra revenues from buying (usually) cheaper imports and selling the grain at (usually) higher domestic prices. Moreover, whenever the government authorises the TMO to export grain, it guarantees any losses incurred (providing what amounts to a variable export subsidy). Such practices give the TMO a decisive advantage over private traders on such transactions and inhibit the rapid development of private commercial channels.

Reduction of input costs

The Turkish government has sought to improve farmers' incomes and yields by subsidising credit and material inputs to farmers. Another aim of such subsidies is to promote the modernisation of Turkish agriculture. Nevertheless, despite relatively high levels of input subsidisation, Turkey still lacks some of the basic technical information and expertise required by a modern agricultural sector.

A wide range of *concessional credit* is offered to farmers, with credit subsidies being the single largest component of input subsidies in the PSE accounts in recent years. Throughout the 1980s, rates on short-term loans have been below market rates of interest and often below the rate of inflation. The Turkish Bank of Agriculture handles the bulk of the credits destined for farmers, ASCUs, processors, commodity brokers and agricultural credit co-operatives. Besides serving as the country's largest commercial bank – accounting for some one-fifth of the deposits and loans in the Turkish banking sector – the bank's statutes require it to use its financial resources in line with the objectives of the Five-Year Development Plans and of the Annual Programmes. Its agricultural support functions include paying input subsidies, disbursing credit to farmers at concessional rates of interest, and providing financing for the institutions commissioned to carry out purchases of supported commodities. Decisions regarding credits granted to the ASCUs are set out in Support Purchase Decrees issued by the government.

Subsidies to farmers for *material inputs* have included rebates on fertilisers and pesticides, and reductions on charges for maintaining and operating irrigation infrastructure. In addition, producers are not charged for the resource value of the water they use. In the early 1980s, the fertiliser subsidies were to some extent given as a form of "compensation" for the implicit tax on agricultural input users resulting from border measures maintained to protect domestic industries engaged in the production of these inputs. For example, in the early 1980s, the State monopoly controlled most of the importation and distribution of agrochemicals, and subsidies were directed at off-setting the costs of high-cost domestic producers. Currently, the market is largely free, and subsidies for use of agrochemicals do not discriminate between domestic and imported sources.

The importance of the effective management of water resources has been emphasised earlier in this report. The drive to expand irrigated areas is a major priority in Turkey. Investments in irrigation and other land improvements have generally averaged between 1½ and 2 per cent of the value of agricultural production. These investments are large compared with those currently being undertaken in other OECD Member countries, reflecting in part the fact that Turkey is at an earlier stage in the development of its natural resources. The type of capital projects already completed in other OECD countries (many of which were built at public expense) are only now coming on stream in Turkey. As in these countries, however, transfers are involved to the extent that the agricultural sector receives benefits in greater proportion to what it is charged. In relation to cropping patterns, such transfers may either accentuate or offset the effects of price supports. In particular, output price supports can lower the social returns on irrigation infrastructure by encouraging the production of low value added crops on irrigated land.

Input subsidies not only distort crop selection but may also adversely affect the environment. Fertiliser subsidies encourage general over-consumption and associated pollution and may encourage a pattern of use that is inappropriate to particular soil-crop combinations. Water subsidies, if not carefully monitored, may lead to waste of water and to agricultural practices that cause excessive soil salinity.[80] Indeed, Turkey's relatively high input subsidies – if they are to contribute to the objective of modernising Turkish agriculture – would seem to require a considerable investment in agricultural research, advisory services and training that has been inadequate to date[81] (see below). In particular, insufficient regional and local data on, for example, soil attributes and livestock feeding needs may mean that farmers are far from the optimal levels and mixes of input use.[82] Ironically, then, while the government has spent large amounts of money for concessional sales of many farm inputs, it has yet to address some of the more obvious needs of the sector. These would include, first and foremost, accumulating the basic data and know-how that would allow the sector to use these inputs effectively.

General service subsidies consist largely of government investments in infrastructure, particularly on-farm irrigation and drainage works; provision of inspection services; expenditure on research and development, advisory services and training. Expenditure on research advisory services and training has generally averaged less than $1/2$ per cent of the value of agricultural production in recent years. This compares with levels of expenditure on research and extension of around 1 per cent in other OECD member countries and is below levels recommended for developing countries by the Food and Agricultural Organisation.[83]

Very recent developments

This discussion of the evolution of agricultural subsidies over the last fourteen years would seem to indicate that Turkey is now poised to repeat other Member countries' mistakes in the area of farm policy. Large amounts of money have been spent on price supports that go to relatively rich farmers or to non-farming players in the agri-food system; at the same time, pressing needs for better social services in rural areas and for better research and extension services have gone unanswered. Problems have emerged as the government attempts to operate an administered price system in place of the market: major inefficiencies occur, the domestic agri-food system fails to develop into a sophisticated, high performance sector capable of making a significant contribution to national wealth, and the administrative complexity of the system escalates over time.

Some of the very recent moves by the government, however, hint at a desire to step back from this path. In August 1993, it published a decree setting out the elements of a new domestic support system for crops purchased by Turkey's Unions of Agricultural Sales Co-operatives (ASCUs). The decree envisages replacing the current system of intervention purchases and border protection with deficiency payments and lower border protection. (Deficiency payments are output subsidies paid by a government. Its unit value is an administratively-determined price minus the domestic market price.) A month later a separate decree was published making cotton the first crop to which the new system will apply. It is intended that the new system will next be extended to tobacco, followed by hazelnuts. More stringent enforcement of area controls on tobacco, tea and hazelnuts is also envisaged. In a separate move designed to improve the functioning of the internal market for grains, the Turkish Grain Board (TMO) began offering storage services, charging farmers (or other market agents) a daily fee until the grain is sold.

These developments are expected to have little immediate effect on agricultural assistance as measured by the percentage PSE nor do they fundamentally alter the broad structure of Turkish agricultural policy. Overall, though, they do represent a first step in the direction of improved market orientation. By beginning to replace intervention purchases with deficiency payments the government has signalled an important change in its approach to supporting producers, one that is expected to benefit consumers, to improve the transfer efficiency of assistance to producers and, perhaps, to foster a market environment that would encourage the development of the institutions and the expertise required in a market-driven agricultural sector.[84]

IV.   Conclusions

The upswing of the Turkish economy gathered further momentum in 1993, the second year of recovery from the stagnation of 1991. Real GNP expanded by an estimated 7 per cent, by far the highest rate achieved among OECD Member countries. GNP growth is projected by the OECD to return to a more sustainable rate of about 5 per cent in 1994 and 1995 on the assumption that the government will take more determined steps to discipline public finances after the local elections in March 1994. Most of the dynamic expansion of domestic demand in 1993 was due to booming household consumption, bolstered by generous wage settlements and easier access to consumer credit. But private investment also picked up sharply, helped by an improved business climate and better industrial capacity utilisation. Prospects of intensified competition stemming from the formation of the customs union with the European Community foreseen for 1995 are expected to sustain private business investment this year and next. In spite of buoyant economic activity, improvement in the labour market situation has been slow, and is likely to remain so, reflecting the persistently strong growth of the labour force as well as ongoing efforts of companies to enhance productivity.

Domestic demand-led expansion brought about a surge in merchandise imports in 1993, and the current external deficit widened to around $5 billion, some 5 per cent of GNP. The expected recovery in foreign markets should give a boost to merchandise exports from now on, though tourism revenues may remain subdued. With the projected slowdown of import growth, the current external deficit will probably decline, to perhaps $4^{1}/_{2}$ to 5 per cent of GNP in 1994 and $3^{1}/_{2}$ per cent in 1995. Current account deficits have been associated with rising foreign indebtedness: the foreign debt stock jumped to above $60 billion at the end of 1993, around 55 per cent of GNP. Whether such a level of indebtedness is sustainable depends largely on the extent to which foreign borrowing is used for the financing of productive investment.

Underlying inflation pressures remained strong with consumer price inflation averaging 66 per cent in 1993, despite a slowdown in import price increases and price restraint imposed on some of the State economic enterprises (SEEs) by the government in the first half of the year. Inflation pressures are bound to remain high in the near future, reinforced by the recent increase in value-added tax rates and unavoidable public sector price adjustments in the wake of worsening financial conditions of the SEEs. Hence, inflation may rise in 1994 before slowing down somewhat in 1995, to a rate which still remains unusually high by OECD – or indeed worldwide – standards. The root cause of the persistently strong inflationary pressures is the large public sector borrowing requirement (PSBR) which increased further in 1993, to more than 16 per cent of GNP. A sustained process of disinflation is contingent upon the government's ability to improve the public-sector financial position substantially. Failure to do so will almost inevitably lead to inflation higher than projected and risks severely impairing the government's credibility and financial market stability as attested to by the instability in foreign exchange and financial markets in January 1994. Although some technical factors were also partly responsible, it could not have occurred in the absence of ample liquidity caused by the excessive public-sector borrowing requirement.

Public sector deficits need to be brought down to levels which would allow the government's financing needs to be met by drawing on private sector savings rather than the ''inflation tax'', which has uncertain incidence on income distribution and, like most forms of taxation, distorts resource allocation. The inflation tax is imposed on the economy through recourse to Central Bank deficit financing. Heavy government reliance on Central Bank borrowing has been the main reason why Turkey has not experienced an explosive growth of government debt, which in normal circumstances would have created irresistible pressure for fiscal correction. Instead, the health of the economy has been undermined gradually but surely through persistently high inflation and interest rates, which have led to a rising share of interest charges in total government spending, thereby limiting the resources available for socially desirable functions such as education. Other manifestations of the malady include a shortening of the planning horizon by companies, distraction of scarce managerial attention to short-term financing arrangements and high-yielding financial engineering, and people's distrust of their own currency. Determined moves towards restoring macro-economic equilibrium are now urgently called for.

As in previous years, monetary policy has been hampered by the huge government financing requirement. As a result, instead of pursuing stabilisation policies the Central Bank has been obliged to confine itself to keeping orderly conditions in financial and foreign exchange markets. One way of increasing the margin of manœuvre for the Central Bank would be to legislate a scheduled reduction in the legal limit on Treasury borrowing, from the current 15 per cent of the government appropriations down to nil over the medium term. This could lead to financing difficulties in the short run. On the other hand, if this is seen as a sign of the government's firm resolve to deal with the problem of public finances, then interest rates could fall, even substantially, generating a momentum for a virtuous circle of lower interest payments helping to reduce fiscal deficits and improve financial conditions for productive investment. But for this to happen the government's programme of deficit reduction must have credibility. Credibility can be gained through charting a medium-term consolidation path and instituting concrete mechanisms – such as spending caps and a sequestration procedure – to ensure the attainment of objectives, but no institutional arrangement is a substitute for actually delivering concrete results. The government aims at reducing the PSBR by some 2 percentage points in 1994. The attainment of this objective should be a minimum first step towards establishing credibility.

To bring about the desirable public sector deficit cut, bold measures are imperative on both revenues and expenditures. The measures taken in 1993 led to a reduction of the primary deficit – which excludes interest payments – by $3^{3}/_{4}$ percentage points. But these measures were grossly insufficient in relation to the huge task of reducing the PSBR. There is a particularly large potential for raising tax revenues, which rose to about 32 per cent of GNP, which remains among the lowest shares in the OECD area. Several steps have already been taken to this effect including the repeated increases in indirect tax rates, the latest being in November 1993. As well, several groups of income earners who had previously been taxed according to the "lump-sump tax system", which regularly led to under-assessment of tax liabilities, have been obliged to file income declarations as from 1993. The Parliament passed a new tax law in December 1993, which addresses several of the deficiencies of the old tax system. The new law reduced the number of exemptions from corporate tax which previously allowed many firms to bring their effective tax rates down to half the statutory rate, thereby keeping the revenues from corporate taxation very low. However, much remains to be done to improve revenue collection and make taxation more equitable. There is also much scope for improving tax administration. Further steps in tax reform would allow not only a narrowing of the government deficit, but also a shifting of the burden of income taxation away from wage earners towards self-employed. Higher revenues would open room for reducing the exceptionally high and distorting (explicit and implicit) taxation of financial transactions, a major source of the wide margin between non-subsidised credit interest rates and bank deposit rates.

On the spending side the room for economy appears substantial with respect both to the number of staff and to remuneration in the public sector. This is attested to by a rather rapid rise in the share of the public sector wage bill in GNP, from $9\frac{1}{4}$ per cent in 1990 to $12\frac{3}{4}$ per cent in 1993. Several measures to contain non-wage spending and caps on wages of seasonal workers (which account for some 10 per cent of the total public-sector wage bill) and on overtime payments for all workers are steps in the right direction. In this context, the stated intention of the government not to grant wage increases below inflation in 1994 seriously impedes efforts to tackle the deficit problem squarely. The recently introduced early retirement scheme may also deserve reassessment, as it not only gives rise to substantial government transfers to the Pension Fund, but also risks wasting scarce and valuable human resources.

More determined action is needed to reform the SEEs, which absorb a sizeable part of government resources, through transfers from the central government budget – $2\frac{1}{2}$ per cent of GNP in 1993 – but also through off-budget assistance in the form of government bonds and implicit transfers by ''deferred debt obligations''. Adding off-budget assistance roughly doubles the burden the SEEs impose on the government. Privatisation is the most desirable strategy for reform of the public enterprise sector, as it widens the scope for private entrepreneurial initiative, which has proved so successful in generating strong economic growth. The government's privatisation programme should be focused primarily on eliminating the waste of resources – indicated by the enormous need of government aid for the SEEs – and enhancing overall efficiency in the economy, rather than just trying to maximise short-run revenues from the sale of SEEs. Workers displaced by rationalisation of the SEEs can draw on the severance payments system as well as on the traditional informal social safety net provided by families and villages. But even if supplementary government assistance were provided to ease individual hardship, it would be less costly over the medium term than carrying on indefinitely with the current system of government support for chronically loss-making SEEs.

Yet another important source of public sector deficits are subsidies to the farm sector, which show up in huge losses of those SEEs which administer the government's agricultural policies – mainly the Turkish Grain Board (TMO), the Sugar Corporation and the Monopoly Administration. As discussed in Chapter III of this Survey, the major effect of policy choices made since the late 1980s has been to increase farm subsidies. Secretariat estimates show that aggregate levels of support – measured as percentage net Producer Subsidy Equivalent (PSE) – have come close to the OECD average, which is high. This represents a doubling of percentage subsidies from their 1979 levels. Since the mid-1980s, policy has shifted toward a greater reliance on market price supports, which accounted for four-fifths of the total PSEs in 1993.

The move toward higher agricultural subsidies should be reversed. Turkey appears to have significant comparative advantage in a wide range of agricultural products and its agri-food sector holds the promise of making an important contribution to its economic development. Heavy subsidies will impede, not facilitate, the development of the sector. They lead to inefficiencies throughout the agri-food sector and prevent the development of sophisticated capabilities in such sub-sectors as agricultural inputs and in the processing and trading of primary products. They are inefficient as the cost of administering the complex system is high and only a small portion of the transfers are likely to accrue to farmers as higher incomes; much is siphoned off by input suppliers and by processors. Furthermore, as in most other OECD countries, a disproportionate share of these subsidies are received by wealthier farm households. This makes output-related farm programmes a very inefficient way of redistributing income toward needier households. OECD experience undoubtedly holds useful lessons for Turkey both as to what might be done and as to what to avoid, as it considers the choices in reforming its own agricultural policies. Finally, in a context of very pressing fiscal constraints, the subsidies also absorb resources that could be put to better use and in particular impose a heavy burden on consumers, many of whom earn lower incomes than in most other OECD countries.

Experience in other OECD countries has shown that such support policies, if left in place for long, lead to changes in all aspects of agricultural production and marketing (production technique, farm diversification, farm finance, regional production patterns), leaving the sector structurally dependent on the subsidies and making it very difficult to dismantle them. If Turkey maintains these high subsidy levels for much longer, it may find it increasingly difficult to reduce them without causing major disruptions in the farm sector.

Turkey has already taken some steps to improve the structure of its agricultural support. The recent initiatives in cotton and tobacco – for which deficiency payments will be offered in conjunction with more stringent enforcement of production controls – represent a positive first step toward putting Turkish agriculture back onto a more solid foundation. This step will have to be followed by others: the government should extend the measure to other products. Support could then be better targeted to needier farmers. It is also desirable to refocus expenditure on basic education for rural populations, on agricultural research and its diffusion and on carefully chosen infrastructure development, especially for irrigation.

As part of this process the Turkish authorities will need to address other policies that directly affect the structure and performance of the agri-food sector. Accelerating the privatisation or liquidation of state-owned enterprises engaged in agricultural support activities and de-regulating markets would generate efficiency gains and improve both the transparency and the transfer efficiency of agri-food policies. Enacting a law on competition – currently under consideration in the Parliament – and applying it to agri-food firms and, in particular, to the agri-food SEEs, may help clarify the ground rules for competition in the sector.

These reforms would complement efforts currently undertaken to bring Turkish trade-related and commercial laws into closer convergence with that of the European Community as part of the preparation for the customs union. The new legislative initiatives encompass the fields of competition policy, state aids, anti-dumping provisions, intellectual property rights, technical regulations concerning industrial products and public procurement, as well as further revisions to the laws on banking and insurance. These moves should not be seen as obligations but rather as opportunities. Once implemented, these reform measures will improve the functioning of the economy and will allow Turkey to take full advantage of the free access to large European markets provided by the customs union.

Notes

1. In 1990, the State Institute of Statistics (SIS) revised the methodology of the national income accounts and started publishing quarterly GNP estimates by kind of activity, with the base year changed from 1968 to 1987. Historical estimates were also revised and new series are now available from 1968 onwards. The revised output series exceed the old ones by some 30 per cent in current prices. Although in 1993, the SIS also prepared new expenditure accounts, there are significant differences between SIS and State Planning Office (SPO) estimates, particularly for deflators and investment estimates. Both SIS and SPO are currently working on a common concept, and it is expected that harmonised new series will be available by March 1994. For the time being, the SPO works with the old series but uses SIS growth rates for the production account. The OECD Secretariat currently follows the SPO because programme targets and annual estimates are still based on the old series. Once the SPO switches to a new concept, the Secretariat will revise all national income statistics.

2. A more detailed discussion is given in the 1992/93 OECD *Economic Survey of Turkey* which devoted a special chapter to the labour market.

3. This is in accordance with the State Institute of Statistics' index of employment in larger manufacturing enterprises which also shows a marked decrease in 1992 and 1993, irrespective of the strong expansion of production. It appears to confirm the observation of labour shedding, hiring of fixed-contract workers who are not covered by collective bargaining agreements and progressive resort to sub-contracting as the employers' response to the "wage explosion" between 1989 and 1991.

4. However, the low 12-monthly price increases for food in early 1993 exaggerate the achieved stabilisation as they were largely the statistical effect of surging prices a year earlier.

5. Crude oil import prices in dollar terms are estimated to have fallen by about 10 per cent in 1993.

6. This scheme was initially established between the Dresdner Bank of Germany and the Central Bank of Turkey to attract deposits of Turkish workers in Germany. The deposit interest rates are determined by the Central Bank of Turkey and the Dresdner Bank acts as an agent of the Central Bank. Turkish nationals living in other countries can also benefit from the scheme and may open foreign exchange deposit accounts directly with the Central Bank of Turkey.

7. The final deficit may even be larger, primarily due to the likely downward revision of non-tax revenues.

8. Here the SEEs include government-owned financial institutions but exclude those SEEs on the privatisation programme.

9. The government decided to integrate 62 EBFs into the consolidated budget as from 1993 – with the exception of the Defence Industry Fund (DIF), the Social Solidarity Fund (SSF) and the Research Fund (RF) – and to liquidate several small funds. Under the new scheme, the EBFs' aggregate revenues are transferred to the consolidated budget, and in turn EBFs are allocated appropriations from the budget, recorded under "transfers". However, for 11 EBFs – including 8 large EBFs – a separate consolidated account was needed as not all of these EBFs' functions were included in the central government accounts.

10. The social security system consists of three main institutions: the Pension Fund for civil servants, the Social Insurance Institution for private sector employees and wage earners in SEEs, and the Bag-Kur for self-employed.

11. Part of the large increase in central government spending, both projection and actual, is attributable to transfers to the EBFs integrated in the consolidated budget. Excluding the EBFs, the increase in total budget spending was around 105 per cent in 1993 as opposed to the projected increase of 60 per cent.

12. The intended domestic borrowing strategy was to extend the maturity of bond issue to at least 12 months (see the 1992/93 OECD *Economic Survey of Turkey,* Annex I). But selling longer-term government paper proved difficult so that borrowing eventually concentrated on three-month and six-month Treasury bills.

13. Under the new legislation women are eligible for retirement after 20 years of work and men after 25 years, regardless of age. Previously the age limit was 50 years for women and 55 years for men.

14. The general VAT rate was raised from 12 to 15 per cent, for basic foodstuffs from 6 to 8 per cent and for luxury goods from 20 to 23 per cent. The Monopoly Administration, as in the past, held back a large part of the tax collected. Therefore, the original government projection of TL 6.5 trillion revenue from this source has been reduced to TL 1 trillion, which eventually might be trimmed down even further.

15. The "expenditure rebate system" was introduced in 1984. At the beginning, the system was designed to reimburse to wage-earners a certain percentage of their expenditure on basic commodities. The aim pursued by this scheme was two-fold:
    – to encourage the formal registration of transactions in the economy (by collecting invoices presented by rebate-seeking individuals) in order to ensure a minimum standard of VAT compliance in a country where tax evasion is believed to be relatively widespread;
    – to reinforce the progressivity of the income tax schedule by means of the regressive structure of the rebate system (the rate of rebate being a decreasing function of expenditure and the maximum amount of expenditure covered being limited to after-tax income).

    Later, the list of the beneficiaries of the system was extended to other taxpayers and the range of the items covered was widened.

16. The expected returns from privatisation in 1994 amount to TL 45 trillion (about \$2.5 billion at the projected exchange rate), of which TL 15 trillion will go to the Public Participation Administration and TL 30 trillion will be allocated to the government budget.

17. The Central Bank law sets a very generous limit to short-term advances to the Treasury at 15 per cent of the central government budget appropriations.

18. Including those in the process of privatisation.

19. Wage contracts for 315 000 workers – almost 90 per cent of total SEE employment – granted pay increases of 37 per cent in the first half of 1993 and 28 per cent in the second half of the year. In 1994, wage adjustments are indexed to consumer price inflation.

20. The Electricity Corporation, the Sugar Corporation and PTT utilise funds collected in the Public Participation Fund under the wage-earners compulsory saving scheme.

21. At the beginning of 1992, the government proposed the establishment of a new institution, the Turkish Autonomisation, Reorganisation and Privatisation Board (TÖYÖK), as the sole authority to enforce the privatisation programme as well as to reorganise those SEEs which were chosen to be maintained or to be liquidated eventually. In fact, TÖYÖK was designed to be given more power and more autonomy than the Public Participation Administration (PPA), which had been in charge of privatisation since 1986, and which TÖYÖK would replace. It was planned to leave management of TÖYÖK to professional administrators, recruited by the government among successful managers in both the private and public sector. However, the TÖYÖK bill has not won the support of the Parliament.

22. For more details on the Central Bank's medium-term approach see the 1990/91 and 1991/92 OECD *Economic Surveys of Turkey,* Chapter II.

23. The 1992 Monetary Programme envisaged an expansion of the Central Bank balance sheet between 37 and 47 per cent, hence below the projected 55 per cent growth of nominal GNP. Growth in the range of 38 to 48 per cent and 27 to 39 per cent for total domestic liabilities and net domestic assets, respectively, were also foreseen for 1992. After an 83 per cent rise in 1991, the rise of the Central Bank money stock (CBM) was projected to slow to a rate between 40 and 50 per cent, which would have been broadly in line with projected inflation during 1992.

24. Previously, the reserve requirement ratios on Turkish lira deposits were 16 per cent for sight deposits and 7.5 per cent for time deposits. For foreign exchange deposits reserve requirement had to be held both in foreign exchange and in Turkish lira. The liquidity requirement ratio was 35 per cent on total deposits, but banks were allowed to hold 70 per cent in interest-bearing government paper. The new "liquidity requirement ratio" is 22 per cent on all liabilities except sight deposits, but including asset-backed investment funds and mutual-investment funds. Of the 22 per cent liquidity requirement 6 percentage points have to be held in Turkish lira, 3 percentage points in foreign currency and 13 percentage points in interest-bearing government paper. However, these new measures were suspended at the beginning of February 1994.

25. For example, Central Bank advances to the Treasury grew at a rate of about 400 per cent in mid-1992.

26. Reserve money is the sum of banknotes issued and net reserves held by commercial banks at the Central Bank.

27. The Central Bank money stock is the sum of reserve money and liabilities to banks arising from open-market operations, unused public-sector credit lines and public-sector deposits.

28. The technique consists of selling bonds with a promise of repurchase at a certain time and at a certain price – or at an imputed interest rate which is usually higher than the relevant deposit rate. These transactions are carried out mostly in government bonds, but also in bank bonds, bank-guaranteed bonds, bonds issued by the Public Participation Administration and local administrations and other bonds registered at the stock exchange. The volume of these ''repo'' transactions expanded by over 200 per cent during the first ten months of 1993.

29. Like time deposits held with banks, government securities are available at maturities of three, six, nine and 12 months, but usually provide a much higher and tax-free return.

30. Note that – for lack of data – M2X does not cover cash holdings of foreign currency.

31. Note that there is no withholding tax on non-banks' interest income from bonds.

32. More precisely, the implicit tax refers only to the reserves in excess of what the banks would in any event hold for prudential reasons.

33. For a presentation of such a model see the 1993 OECD *Economic Survey of Hungary,* Annex IV. The analysis suggests that the inflation sensitivity of the spread between lending and borrowing interest rate grows with a rising proportion of non-performing loans in the banks' assets, a higher reserve requirement ratio, a rising deposit share in bank assets and a higher capital-to-asset ratio.

34. However, insofar as relative wholesale prices are a better indicator for international price competitiveness, the above quoted figures exaggerate the real effective appreciation of the Turkish lira. This is so because in recent years, Turkish wholesale price inflation was markedly lower – some 8 percentage points in 1992 – than consumer price inflation and this negative differential was larger in Turkey than in the average of trading partner countries.

35. A typical example of such a model is to take the share of foreign currency deposits in broad money (M2X) as indicator of currency substitution and explain the change of this variable by the domestic-foreign interest rate differential and exchange rate expectations. The expected exchange rate has often been proxied by differences between domestic and foreign inflation rates. However, estimates of a quarterly model by the Secretariat using three-month money market interest rates and as foreign variables the weighted averages of the respective US and German series failed to capture interest and exchange rate effects simultaneously. It proved possible to separately identify statistically significant interest- or inflation differential effects on the foreign exchange deposit-M2X ratio, but not both. For example, the decline in currency substitution from the third quarter of 1988 to the second quarter of 1990, as shown in Diagram 8, is attributable to the unusual deviation of both domestic-foreign interest and inflation differentials from their averages during this period.

36. For a discussion of these issues see, for example, Calvo and Végh (1992).

37. Currently, the reserve requirement on sight deposits in foreign currency is 17.5 per cent as opposed to 16.0 per cent on Turkish lira sight deposits. 9.5 percentage points of the former are to be held in foreign exchange and 8 percentage points in lira. The reserve requirement on foreign exchange time deposits is 14.5 per cent and the foreign exchange/lira composition is 11.5/3.0 percentage points, respectively.

38. In the case where foreign money fulfilled all the monetary needs of the public, the revenue raised through the inflation tax would be zero, and monetary financing would disappear as a means of financing the fiscal deficit. A very close approximation to a fully "dollarised" economy is Panama, where annual average inflation during the 1980s was below 2 per cent.

39. The exact meaning of the term "seigniorage" is subject to a variety of interpretations in the literature. One alternative concept, for example, is that of "opportunity-cost" seigniorage, which is what additional real income individuals would have earned if they had held interest-earning assets instead of non-interest earning money. Estimates of opportunity-cost seigniorage depend crucially on the rate of return used in its calculation. The analysis is further complicated by structural breaks in Turkish interest-rate series due to past administrative regulations. The estimates shown in Table 19 suggest that since 1981 opportunity-cost seigniorage exceeds monetary seigniorage by a substantial margin.

40. In line with the above definition, the inflation tax equals the rate of inflation multiplied by the reserve money/GNP ratio. This implies that seigniorage and inflation tax are identical when the rate of reserve money growth equals the inflation rate.

41. Using SEIGN for seigniorage revenues and DCPI for consumer price inflation, the following regression has been run on yearly data from 1974 to 1992, applying the Cochrane-Orcutt correction for first order autocorrelation (*t*-values are in brackets):

$$SEIGN = 0.24751 + 0.10107 \ DCPI - 0.00075 \ (DCPI)^2$$
$$(0.211) \quad\ (2.837) \qquad\quad (2.962)$$

$$S.E.E. = 0.619 \quad D.W. = 1.589 \quad R^2 = 0.372$$

42. Following Rodrik (1991), the model assumes that fiscal deficits are financed *at the margin* exclusively by seigniorage and that other sources of financing do not respond systematically to the deficit. Moreover, the growth of demand for reserve money is determined by a linear combination of real output growth and GNP inflation. With PSBR denoting the public sector borrowing requirement, DGNPV the growth rate of real GNP, DPGNP the change in the GNP deflator and M the reserve money stock, ordinary-least-squares regression on annual data from 1978 to 1993 results in (t-values are in brackets):

$$DPGNP = 51.668 + 15.230 \ (PSBR/M) - 3.216 \ DGNPV$$
$$(5.59) \quad\ (2.29) \qquad\qquad (2.42)$$

$$D.W. = 2.02 \quad S.E.E. = 15.46 \quad R^2 = 0.46$$

43. In general, the *ceteris paribus* clause is – of course – unrealistic. Hence, one would expect a reduction of the PSBR/GNP ratio to have an effect on total demand and output. However, past experience shows that in Turkey changes in the PSBR were accompanied by offsetting movements in private saving (see Diagram 3 of the 1991/1992 OECD *Economic Survey of Turkey*, Chapter I). But even if a government expenditure multiplier of 1, for example, were assumed, the effect on inflation of a reduction in the PSBR stemming from a contraction of real GNP would take away from the overall disinflation effect gauged above only one-fifth (*i.e.* a 1 percentage point reduction in the PSBR/GNP ratio would induce GNP inflation to fall by 12 rather than 15 percentage points).

44. World Bank (1993), *World Development Report,* page 298-299.

45. According to World Bank figures, which use a slightly different statistical category, Turkey averaged 58 deaths per 1 000 live births in 1991. This compares with an average of 38 for middle income developing countries and 34 for upper-middle income developing countries. *World Bank Development Report,* 1993.

46. These include not only the health services that are responsible for reaching at-risk children, but also those responsible for water quality and for education, particularly of women.

47. See OECD, *Regional Problems and Policies in Turkey,* Paris, 1988.

48. OECD, ''Farm employment and economic adjustment in OECD countries'', forthcoming.

49. The General Agricultural Census (1991) shows that the highest average cultivated area per household engaged in agriculture is 8.2 hectares in central north Anatolia, while the lowest average cultivated area per household is 2.4 hectares in the Black Sea provinces.

50. This compares with 27 hectares for France (1985), 4.3 hectares for Greece (1985), 3 700 hectares for Australia (1991), and 190 hectares for the United States (1991).

51. It should be noted that the problem of fragmentation of ownership does not necessarily imply fragmented operation. Some farmers operate holdings on behalf of absent family owners or under rental arrangements. Data on this and other aspects of farm structure are scarce.

52. The large number of multi-parcel agricultural land holdings in Turkey is in part a consequence of the 1926 Civil Code, which is patterned after the Swiss Civil Code. The inheritance provisions of this law specify that, upon the death of a landowner, 25 per cent of the land should pass to the owner's spouse (if still alive) and the rest should be distributed equally among the surviving children.

53. It should be noted, however, that land consolidation has occurred in countries with similar inheritance laws and similar attitudes towards land ownership.

54. Other sources of growth have been increases in double cropping and some expansion in the area sown.

55. Yields in Europe are very high for several reasons. Because of relative factor endowments (especially relatively low cultivable land area per capita) European farming systems tend to be more intensive. This is reinforced by agricultural price supports that provide strong incentives to increase yields through the intensive use of yield-enhancing inputs such as fertilisers and insecticides.

56. Turkey's population density (70 inhabitants per square kilometre) is one of the lowest in Europe and is similar to that of Spain (78 inhabitants per square kilometre).

57. Regional yield differences in Turkey are large. Average cereals yields in the Marmara region, for example, are two to three times those of the Van region in the South-east. This reflects not only differences in agro-climatic conditions but in the technological sophistication of agricultural practices (*Agriculture Structure and Production,* State Institute of Statistics, Ankara, 1989).

58. These are the General Directorate of State Hydraulic Works (DSI) and the General Directorate of Rural Services. The DSI is responsible for major irrigation, flood control, swamp reclamation, hydropower development and supplying water to cities with populations exceeding 100 000 people. Works inside the farm gate are the responsibility of the General

Directorate of Rural Services, which is also responsible for rural roads, village water supply, minor irrigation and on-farm development.

59. Those irrigation projects currently under construction are not expected to be completed before the end of the decade. When they are completed, only 18 per cent of the targeted irrigated area for the total project will be covered.

60. This study is based on an Irrigation Master Plan questionnaire.

61. Another reason cited, although by many fewer respondents, was the lack of private facilities needed to make irrigation possible on the farm.

62. The World Bank irrigation report identifies several problems associated with operations and maintenance management. First, there is no relationship between operation and maintenance funding and tariff recovery: whether a high or a low percentage of assessments is recovered in a region, the operation and maintenance allocation for the region is not affected. Second, there is no accountability or control for collectors who do not collect and for farmers who do not pay. Furthermore, because the government is authorised to make reductions to irrigation fees, they are often set lower than the fee schedule indicated by DSI.

63. The estimates indicate that the domestic resource costs for a variety of products are well under their respective world prices. The lowest is for olive oil, where the calculations indicate that domestic resource cost is only 10 per cent of the world price. Other calculations are for wheat (40 per cent), barley (34 per cent), corn (63 per cent), tobacco (21 per cent), sugar beet (101 per cent), tomatoes (12 per cent) and melons (17 per cent). *Turkey: Review of Agricultural Pricing and Trade Policies,* October 1990, World Bank Report No. 7764-TU.

64. For a variety of reasons, these transfers cannot be interpreted as monetary flows that necessarily give rise to increased welfare for farmers relative to what they would have had in the absence of support policies. First, they may be dissipated by production inefficiencies. Second, they may accrue to vertically related industries such as input suppliers or downstream buyers.

65. These have been calculated by the Agricultural Directorate of the OECD – in collaboration with the Turkish authorities – as part of its recent review of agricultural policies in Turkey. These calculations and related analysis are to be published in ''National Policies and Agricultural Trade: Country Study of Turkey'', forthcoming.

66. PSE for a given support measure represents the value of the transfer by consumers and taxpayers to agricultural producers due to the measure, and in respect of the existing level of production of the product in question.

67. Only about two-fifths of overall Turkish agricultural production is included in the set of standard commodities for which Producer and Consumer Subsidy Equivalents (PSEs and CSEs) are calculated, the lowest share across all OECD countries. However, virtually all of the major commodities excluded from the PSE/CSE measure benefit from input and infrastructure subsidies and several, including hazelnuts, tobacco and tea, are covered by support purchase schemes.

68. Subsidies offered *via* under-pricing of the resource value of water used for irrigation purposes are not included in any of the PSE calculations, although such subsidies are common in

the arid agricultural zones of the OECD. An estimate of transfers offered in the form of subsidies for irrigation infrastructure development is included.

69. The CSE represents the consumer tax equivalent net of any consumer subsidies resulting from the measure under consideration, *i.e.* the net values of the consumer transfers to agricultural producers in respect of the existing level of consumption of the given product.

70. ASCUs (Agricultural Sales Cooperatives Unions) are commercial organisations established under a special law. They are authorised to set prices for the members' commodities "in the best possible conditions". When commissioned by the government, they may implement support purchases from producers on behalf of the State. The ASCUs are also authorised to set up facilities such as warehouses, primary processing and packaging plants and to market commodities. An ASCU can be established through association of at least three agricultural sales cooperatives. As of 1993, there were 17 ASCUs operating in various regions across the country with a total of 387 member co-operatives and nearly 685 000 individual members; seven or eight of the largest ASCU carry out the bulk of the ASCUs' support purchasing activities.

71. Some (such as TMO) probably have little value as ongoing concerns, since their role has been purely one of implementing agricultural policy. Most of the others play mixed commercial and political roles and may have considerable value – depending on clarification of market regulation and treatment of labour redundancies.

72. See "Technical Change, Structural Adjustment and the Transfer Efficiency of Agricultural Policy", document AGR/CA/APM(93)11.

73. Note that this list is considerably more extensive than an equivalent list would be for the other countries providing extensive agricultural subsidies in the OECD area. In other countries, only a relatively limited number of mainly temperate zone products have been the targets of support policies.

74. As of 1985, tea support operations have been conducted under a somewhat different legal framework than those for most other supported commodities.

75. Aside from the tobacco it purchases to cover the needs of its own cigarette factories, TEKEL is legally obliged to buy all tobacco not sold to private buyers and to stockpile what it cannot sell. In recent years this stockpile has grown considerably and, as of November 1993, had reached approximately half a million tonnes of mainly low grade domestic tobacco from the south-east.

76. Three crops are covered by regulations limiting area planted: hazelnuts (since June 1983), tobacco (since August 1986) and tea (since 1987). Authority for enforcing these controls is vested respectively in the hazelnut grower co-operative (FISKOBIRLIK), the Tobacco Production Board and CAYKUR. In theory, a grower wishing to develop a new plantation or to expand an existing one must first obtain a permit. In practice, compliance with these controls has been sporadic at best, due to ineffective enforcement and pressures from local authorities to continue expansion of output in their areas.

77. Selected self-sufficiency ratios for 1980-82 and for 1990-92 are given below:

Commodity	1980-82	1990-92	Commodity	1980-82	1990-92
Wheat	145	114	Barley	106	112
Maize	100	95	Rice	n.a.	46
Sugarbeet	122	100	Milk	99	95
Beef	104	86	Sheepmeat	125	110

Source: Data based on statistics provided by the State Planning Organisation.

78. Until the mid-1980s, TMO had an exclusive right to import wheat, rye, barley, sorghum and oats. Similarly, permits were required for the import of rice, rapeseed, sunflower seeds, long-staple cotton, and merino wool. Imports of many products – including hazelnuts, raisins, pistachios, dried figs, olive oil, milk powder, beef or veal, sheepmeat, poultry meat and eggs – were prohibited. With few exceptions (wheat, maize, sugar and milk powder still require permits), the quantitative controls or bans have been eliminated.

79. Article 33 of the Additional Protocol states that "Over a period of 22 years Turkey shall adjust its agricultural policy with a view to adopting, at the end of that period, those measures of the common agricultural policy which must be applied in Turkey if free movement of agricultural products between it and the Community is to be achieved".

80. A recent OECD report, *Environmental policies in Turkey,* Paris, 1992, identified both salinisation and pollution by agricultural chemicals as problems that need to be addressed.

81. Turkey lacks a detailed soil map and little research has been performed on the suitability of hybrid varieties of plants and animals to Turkey's agronomic conditions. With regard to subsistence and semi-subsistence agriculture, agriculture technologies have little attraction if they are not suited to the capacity of farmers to furnish capital, labour and purchased inputs and if they imply excessive risks for families whose incomes are marginal. Little is known about the economics of agricultural production in this kind of farm household in Turkey. See Graeme Donovan (1987), "Broadening Production Increase Programmes to reach Low-Income Farmers" in *Food Policy: Integrating Supply, Distribution and Consumption,* edited by J. Price Gittinger, Joanne Leslie and Caroline Hoisington. EDI Series on Economic Development. World Bank, 1987.

82. See Kadir Günay, *Some Observations and Suggestions on the Fertiliser Industry,* unpublished mimeo, March 1991. This report documents the degree to which most types of fertiliser are inefficiently used in Turkey.

83. Donovan, G. *Ibid.*

84. These institutions would include sophisticated commodities exchanges and accompanying systems for product grading and standards as well as private expertise in trading transport and logistics.

References

Aksoy, S. and M. Talim (1989), "Les structures agricoles", in: *Agricultures Méditerranéennes: La Turquie,* Y. Tekelioglu (ed.), Institut Agronomique Méditerranéen de Montpellier, Montpellier.

Altan, F. (1987), *Class Stratification in Agriculture,* Istanbul University doctoral thesis, Istanbul.

Calvo, G.A., and C.A. Végh (1992), "Currency Substitution in Developing Countries: An Introduction", *IMF Working Paper,* International Monetary Fund, Washington (D.C.), May.

Donovan, G. (1987), "Broadening Production Increase Programmes to Reach Low-Income Farmers", in: Gittinger, J.P., J. Leslie and C. Hoisington (eds.), *Food Policy: Integrating Supply, Distribution and Consumption,* EDI Series on Economic Development, World Bank, Washington D.C.

Günay, K. (1991), *Some Observations and Suggestions on the Fertiliser Industry,* unpublished mimeo, Ankara, March.

OECD, *Economic Surveys of Turkey,* Paris, various years.

OECD (1988), *Regional Problems and Policies in Turkey,* Paris.

OECD (1992), *Environmental Policies in Turkey,* Paris.

OECD (1993), *Economic Survey of Hungary,* Paris.

OECD, *Farm Employment and Economic Adjustment in OECD Countries,* forthcoming.

OECD, *National Policies and Agricultural Trade: Country Study of Turkey,* forthcoming.

Rodrik, D. (1991), "Premature Liberalisation, Incomplete Stabilization: The Özal Decade in Turkey", in: M. Bruno *et al.* (eds.), *Lessons of Economic Stabilization and its Aftermath,* MIT Press, Cambridge, Mass.

State Institute of Statistics (1989), *Agriculture Structure and Production,* Ankara.

State Institute of Statistics (1992), *1991 General Census of Agriculture: Results of Village Information Survey.*

World Bank (1990), *Turkey: Review of Agricultural Pricing and Trade Policies,* World Bank Report No. 7764-TU, Washington D.C.

World Bank (1993), *World Development Report,* Washington D.C.

Calendar of main economic events

1993

January

The 1993 investment incentive measures are announced. TL 22 trillion will be allocated to investment incentives, of which TL 15 trillion will be financed from the central government budget. In addition to the Development Bank, commercial banks and other investment banks determined by the Treasury will be involved in the distribution of incentive funds. For the first time, the incentive scheme also includes cultural activities. Regardless of regions, large investment projects exceeding $100 million will be given special treatment.

All public agencies, including municipalities, are required to obtain approval of the Treasury before borrowing from international markets.

Regulations concerning the issue of securities by private companies, State economic enterprises and local administrations are amended. The ceilings on the securities to be issued are to be confined to new debt/capital ratios. The new regulations grant more favourable terms to joint-stock companies open to public participation.

March

The Free-zone Administration Decree is published. In addition to special incentives granted for off-shore operations, firms in the free-zone areas will also benefit from the domestic incentive scheme.

Credit allocations from the Resource Utilisation Support Fund are rearranged. Investments in organised industrial sites without incentive certificates are accorded to benefit from subsidised credits from the Resource Utilisation Support Fund. Unfinished investments in the tourism sector will be given additional credits.

April

New rules concerning gold exports and imports, and capital transfers are published. Gold exports and imports are liberalised. A gold-exchange market will be formed and gold will be traded by authorised institutions. The Turkish lira value of gold will no longer be determined by the Central Bank.

Several restrictions on financial investment by Turkish residents in foreign countries are abolished.

The Petroleum-Price-Stability-Fund surcharges on crude oil and petroleum products are raised from 5 to 10 per cent.

May

The official support price for wheat is increased by an average of 70 per cent.

The subsidised housing credit scheme from the Housing Fund is opened for individual houses outside the mass-housing construction scheme. Unfinished projects will be given additional credits.

June

The opening of a foreign-currency deposit account with a letter of credit at the Central Bank is restricted to Turkish nationals working abroad only, *i.e.* Turkish residents are excluded.

July

Minimum wages in industry, services and agriculture are increased from TL 1.5 million to TL 2.5 million per month.

The civil servants' salary adjustment system is revised. Instead of semi-annual increases, salaries will be raised on a quarterly basis. For the period of July, August and September salaries are increased by 15 per cent.

New rules concerning venture capital companies are announced. The venture capital companies will be joint-stock companies with a minimum capital of TL 300 billion. They will provide interest-free long-term funds through capital market institutions. They are exempt from income and corporation tax. Another decree introduces new regulations which make more transparent the joint-stock companies open to public participation.

The Sümerbank is reorganised by detaching banking and textile manufacturing as separate institutions; the banking section is taken over by the Treasury in order to be privatised immediately.

August

The support price scheme for cotton is changed from the intervention price system to a deficiency payment system. Under the new system, cotton producers will be reimbursed the difference between the price set by the government and the market price.

With a decree published by the Capital Market Board, the establishment of investment funds indexed to the Istanbul Stock Exchange index are allowed.

September

The official support price for sugarbeet is raised by an average of 52 per cent.

The Ministry of Energy and Natural Resources is authorised by the government to privatise the Turkish Electricity Board (TEK). Both public and private institutions operating in the distribution of electricity are requested to allocate up to 10 per cent of their sales revenues to the Electricity Fund which will be utilised in energy investments.

The telecommunications part of the PTT is reorganised as a separate company in order to be privatised.

The banking law is amended in order to bring the Turkish banking system into line with the EC banking system. The new regulations introduce more control on the operations of commercial banks.

November

Value-added tax (VAT) rates are altered; new rates are applicable from 1st November 1993. The general VAT rate is raised from 12 to 15 per cent, on luxury goods from 20 to 23 per cent, and on basic food stuffs from 6 to 8 per cent.

Two extra-budgetary funds, the Public Participation Administration and the Housing Fund are authorised to issue asset-backed securities.

Foreign investment trusts operating in the Istanbul Stock Exchange are granted tax exemptions.

The government's decree concerning the privatisation of the telecommunication part of PTT is countermanded by the Constitutional Court.

December

The 1994 budget is approved by Parliament.

New tax measures are approved by Parliament. The lowest bracket of the income tax schedule is raised from TL 32 million to TL 75 million and the maximum tax rate raised from 50 to 55 per cent. Discriminatory tax rates for priority development regions are abolished. The advance-tax rate is increased from 30 to 50 per cent for personal income tax, and from 50 to 70 per cent for corporation tax. Special deductions from the tax base are increased fourfold and wage earners are allowed to deduct certain expenditures from the tax base. Lump-sum tax rates are raised with the exception of the lowest rate. Lump-sum tax payers are offered a cut in their tax liabilities by half during three years if they switch from the lump-sum system to the income declaration system. The withholding tax on interest income will be kept unchanged in general until 1997. After that date, interest earnings will be included in income declarations but only the real (inflation-adjusted) part of incomes will be subject to taxation. The government is authorised to impose a 5 per cent withholding tax (the previous rate was 10 per cent) on interest income from Turkish lira deposits, government securities and repo transactions. The withholding tax on interest income from foreign-currency deposits, on yields from asset-backed securities, on private sector bonds and on revenue-sharing certificates will be 10 per cent. Dividend income exceeding TL 225 million will be included in income declarations. The corporation tax rate is cut from 46 to 25 per cent and several exemptions are abolished, but the minimum effective tax rate after exemptions must not be less than 20 per cent. In addition to the corporation tax there will be a 20 per cent income tax on distributed profits. For corporations open to public, the rate is 10 per cent. Value-added tax exemptions on projects with special incentives are abolished. The motor vehicle tax is raised by 70 per cent and the motor vehicle purchase tax by 100 per cent.

The 1994 import regime is announced. Customs tariffs and Housing Fund surcharges on several goods imported from the EC are lowered, but surcharges on motor vehicles imported from non-EC countries are raised.

1994

January

In the course of unusual unrest in financial and foreign exchange markets, the Turkish lira depreciates by 13.6 per cent.

Central Bank rediscount rate is revised from 48 to 50 per cent and advance rate from 54.5 to 65 per cent.

The legal reserve requirement and the liquidity ratio are unified to a single "liquidity requirement ratio" and its coverage extended to non-deposit liabilities. Previously, the reserve requirement ratios on Turkish lira deposits were 16 per cent for sight deposits and 7.5 per cent for time deposits. For foreign exchange deposits reserve requirement had to be held both in foreign exchange and in Turkish lira. The liquidity requirement ratio was 35 per cent on total deposits, but banks were allowed to hold 70 per cent in interest-bearing government paper. The new "liquidity requirement ratio" is 22 per cent on all liabilities except sight deposits, but including asset-backed investment funds and mutual-investment funds. Of the 22 per cent liquidity requirement 6 percentage points have to be held in Turkish lira, 3 percentage points in foreign currency and 13 percentage points in interest-bearing government paper.

February

Suspension of 5 per cent transaction tax on government bonds and on repo transactions, which was introduced in January 1994.

New liquidity ratio, which was introduced in January, is also suspended.

STATISTICAL AND STRUCTURAL ANNEX

Table A. **National product** (old series)

TL billion

	1982	1983	1984	1985	1986	1987	1988	1989	1990
					Current prices				
Agriculture, forestry, fishing	1 679	2 118	3 397	4 790	6 586	9 532	16 023	25 366	45 612
Industry	2 192	3 096	5 110	8 061	11 353	16 848	29 727	47 609	73 742
Construction	357	448	697	951	1 411	2 152	3 563	6 013	10 091
Wholesale and retail trade	1 370	1 907	3 140	4 397	6 093	9 326	16 143	26 973	44 563
Transports and communications	842	1 136	1 785	2 711	3 662	5 323	9 308	15 556	25 589
Financial institutions	157	203	467	740	1 027	1 468	2 596	4 660	9 617
Ownership of dwellings	352	450	726	1 056	1 509	2 208	4 074	7 317	12 500
Private professions and services	446	598	971	1 380	1 914	2 852	4 980	8 329	13 866
Government, health, education	687	861	1 057	1 441	2 073	3 219	5 327	9 666	16 153
Gross domestic product at factor costs	8 081	10 817	17 349	25 526	35 628	52 929	91 741	151 488	251 732
Net income from abroad	115	20	163	245	82	266	–244	2 955	4 067
Indirect taxes minus subsidies	540	714	863	2 026	3 660	5 371	9 085	15 969	31 455
Gross national product at market prices	8 735	11 552	18 375	27 797	39 370	58 565	100 582	170 413	287 254
					Percentage volume change, 1968 prices				
Agriculture, forestry, fishing	6.4	–0.2	3.5	2.4	8.0	2.0	8.2	–10.9	11.6
Industry	4.8	8.0	10.1	6.2	8.8	9.5	3.2	3.1	9.0
Construction	0.8	0.8	1.5	3.0	8.8	6.7	1.9	1.2	1.2
Wholesale and retail trade	4.6	6.8	8.0	4.7	9.6	9.8	3.7	6.1	12.8
Transports and communications	2.1	3.1	7.6	4.7	4.5	6.5	3.2	2.4	2.7
Financial institutions	2.0	0.0	5.8	1.8	5.4	3.4	3.3	3.2	4.6
Ownership of dwellings	2.9	2.9	2.8	1.8	3.5	4.3	4.1	3.9	4.5
Private professions and services	4.1	3.9	5.7	5.4	8.5	7.0	4.4	0.0	9.1
Government, health, education	5.1	4.4	2.6	3.3	3.6	4.7	6.3	6.6	3.6
Gross domestic product at factor costs	4.5	3.9	6.0	4.1	7.4	6.4	4.7	0.6	8.2
Gross national product at market prices	4.5	3.3	5.9	5.1	8.1	7.5	3.6	1.9	9.2

Source: State Institute of Statistics and State Planning Organisation, *Main Economic Indicators.*

116

Table A *(cont'd).* **Gross national product** (new series)[1]

TL billion

	Current prices	Constant 1987 prices	% growth
1980	5 362	50 680	−2.3
1981	8 040	53 377	5.3
1982	10 699	55 371	3.7
1983	14 111	57 901	4.6
1984	22 716	62 401	7.8
1985	35 975	65 189	4.5
1986	52 064	70 092	7.5
1987	76 613	76 613	9.3
1988	134 060	77 800	1.5
1989	235 305	78 469	0.9
1990	395 335	86 145	9.8
1991	622 563	86 534	0.5
1992	1 072 114	91 671	5.9

1. In 1990, the State Institute of Statistics (SIS) revised the methodology of the national income accounts and started publishing quarterly GNP estimates by kind of activity, with the base year changed from 1968 to 1987. Historical estimates were also revised and new series are now available from 1972 onwards. The revised ouput series exceed the old ones by some 30 per cent in current prices. Although in 1993 the SIS also prepared new expenditures accounts, there are significant differences between SIS and State Planning Office (SPO) estimates, particularly for deflators and investment estimates. Both SIS and SPO are currently working on a common concept, and it is expected that harmonised new series will be avalaible by March 1994.

Source: State Institute of Statistics and State Planning Organisation, *Main Economic Indicators.*

Table B. **Supply and use of resources**

Percentage volume change over previous year

	1981	1982	1983	1984	1985	1986	1987	1988	1989	1990	1991
Gross national product at market prices	4.1	4.5	3.3	5.9	5.1	8.1	7.5	3.6	1.9	9.2	0.5
Foreign balance [1]	-2.5	-1.7	-1.3	-0.6	-0.7	-3.3	-1.3	-3.2	-0.6	-6.5	2.8
Total domestic demand	1.6	2.8	4.7	5.2	4.4	11.4	6.0	0.4	2.5	16.0	-2.2
Fixed capital investment	1.7	3.5	3.0	0.4	16.9	11.0	5.4	-1.3	-1.0	13.9	-0.2
Public	9.4	2.2	1.9	-4.7	23.1	7.5	-3.7	-13.7	-5.8	8.0	4.5
Private	-8.7	5.5	4.7	8.4	8.2	16.4	18.6	13.5	3.3	18.8	-3.0
Stock changes [1]	-0.8	-1.0	-0.2	-0.4	-0.6	-0.6	-0.1	-1.3	-0.2	4.1	-3.9
Consumption	0.6	3.9	4.7	6.2	1.5	10.9	6.3	2.7	4.1	11.2	1.9
Public	0.9	2.0	1.7	2.1	3.1	6.6	3.8	1.9	3.3	7.0	2.5
Private	0.6	4.2	5.0	6.8	1.3	11.5	6.6	2.8	4.2	10.4	1.8

1. Contribution to GNP growth.
Source: State Planning Organisation, *Main Economic Indicators*.

Table C. **Industrial production**

Percentage changes over previous year, volume
Index 1986 = 100, value-added weighted

	1987	1988	1989	1990	1991	1992	1993	
							Q1	Q2
Total industry	10.5	1.6	3.7	9.5	2.6	5.0	2.5	12.4
Public	12.8	3.0	0.9	7.9	3.9	3.8	4.0	6.1
Private	8.7	0.5	6.0	10.6	1.6	6.0	1.2	17.3
Mining	5.1	−5.2	12.6	6.0	10.1	−3.0	−10.8	−10.3
Public	7.2	−6.4	17.2	13.1	13.7	−3.4	−8.1	−10.9
Private	0.2	−2.2	1.6	−13.5	−2.7	−1.1	−21.8	−7.5
Energy	11.7	8.4	8.1	10.8	3.8	12.2	8.0	11.4
Public	11.9	8.3	10.4	11.4	5.1	10.8	8.6	10.1
Private	10.6	7.8	−10.3	3.8	−10.4	29.8	1.0	23.2
Manufacturing	10.7	0.9	2.1	9.5	1.8	4.2	2.3	14.3
Public	14.0	2.1	−5.5	5.5	1.5	1.2	3.4	7.0
Private	8.9	0.4	6.6	11.6	1.9	5.7	1.7	17.6
of which:								
Foods, beverages, tobacco	3.5	4.5	6.7	6.8	9.2	−3.6	−5.7	8.5
Public	−1.0	3.1	2.8	3.1	11.5	−5.9	−9.1	15.6
Private	9.5	6.3	11.0	10.9	6.8	−1.2	−1.5	2.5
Textile, clothing, leather	8.4	1.8	3.2	2.3	−8.6	4.3	0.1	6.2
Public	18.7	−8.5	−15.4	20.2	−24.3	−7.3	−6.5	−3.3
Private	7.0	3.5	5.5	0.4	−6.6	5.5	0.6	7.1
Forestry products	4.4	−2.8	2.0	17.4	−6.2	0.6	−12.2	5.7
Public	−5.4	6.6	1.9	6.8	−6.7	−5.2	−29.7	−2.3
Private	10.4	−7.8	2.2	23.8	−6.0	3.7	−2.3	9.0
Paper and printing	14.1	−7.3	2.6	15.3	−5.9	9.8	8.6	13.8
Public	15.4	−26.6	20.5	11.0	−13.3	14.0	−10.1	−21.2
Private	13.7	−1.2	−1.5	16.4	−4.0	8.8	13.6	22.9
Chemicals, petroleum	15.1	2.6	0.4	3.3	−0.6	3.2	5.9	11.6
Public	24.9	6.2	−8.8	1.6	−1.1	4.6	11.8	7.4
Private	6.0	−1.1	11.5	4.9	−0.2	2.0	0.6	15.5
Soil products	12.9	6.1	4.7	3.8	4.6	11.7	−7.7	1.8
Public	14.1	−4.3	10.1	−4.2	12.9	5.7	−37.5	−30.7
Private	12.7	8.0	3.9	5.2	3.3	12.7	−5.1	7.6
Basic metals	12.1	−0.2	1.2	16.8	−7.8	6.5	14.9	20.6
Public	2.9	3.0	−15.4	30.9	−7.6	1.1	20.3	6.9
Private	18.6	−2.1	12.0	9.9	−7.9	9.6	11.8	29.2
Machinery and transport equipment	8.5	−6.7	−1.2	31.8	11.8	8.1	1.9	31.4
Public	8.1	−28.6	−0.6	23.2	15.2	5.5	−10.0	12.5
Private	8.5	−4.4	−1.3	32.6	11.5	8.4	2.7	32.8
Other manufacturing	11.4	−17.4	72.9	34.3	−22.7	40.7	28.8	62.0
Public	96.6	24.6	87.6	−17.9	44.7	75.9	−0.5	41.2
Private	9.8	−18.9	72.1	37.3	−25.0	38.4	30.0	63.9

Source: State Institute of Statistics, *Quarterly Industrial Production Index.*

Table D. **Prices**[1]

Percentage change over previous year, annual averages

	Wholesale prices							Consumer prices	
	General index			Agriculture	Mining	Manufacturing industry	Energy	General	Food
	Total	Public	Private						
Old series (Weights)	Base year 1981 = 100, 1981 weights							Base year 1978-79 = 100	
	(100)	(28.55)	(71.45)	(30.39)	(2.98)	(64.25)	(2.38)	(100)	(45.30)
1982	27.0	28.8	26.3	24.5	49.3	26.5	45.7	34.1	29.7
1983	30.5	27.3	31.7	31.2	20.5	31.2	25.7	31.4	26.0
1984	50.3	47.7	51.4	57.5	41.2	46.5	75.3	48.4	57.1
1985	43.2	53.8	39.1	37.4	63.9	41.9	97.6	45.0	40.6
1986	29.6	27.6	30.4	25.3	13.6	32.6	35.6	34.6	30.4
1987	32.0	23.1	35.8	29.6	35.7	33.6	23.4	38.9	39.8
1988	68.3	68.9	68.1	51.0	70.0	77.8	40.2	75.4	71.1
1989	69.6	67.9	70.2	81.4	84.1	64.6	66.0	69.6	70.6
New series (Weights)	Base year 1987 = 100, 1987 weights							Base year 1987 = 100	
	(100)	(27.74)	(72.26)	(23.03)	(2.54)	(69.80)	(4.62)	(100)	(32.10)
1988	70.5	70.3	70.5	44.1	64.1	81.5	40.9	73.7	83.2
1989	64.0	64.2	63.9	71.7	65.0	61.6	69.2	63.2	69.3
1990	52.3	56.7	50.6	70.6	48.7	46.9	56.5	60.3	64.3
1991	55.3	61.3	53.0	50.8	63.2	55.3	75.1	66.0	67.1
1992	62.1	65.2	60.8	62.7	60.3	59.7	97.7	70.1	71.3
1993	58.4	54.5	60.1	62.2	56.7	56.6	67.8	66.1	63.5

1. In January 1990, the State Institute of Statistics introduced new weights for both wholesale and consumer prices indices, and shifted the base year of the consumer price index from 1978-79 to 1987. In January 1991, the base year for the wholesale index is shifted from 1981 to 1987.

Source: State Institute of Statistics, *Price Indices Monthly Bulletin.*

Table E. Imports by commodities [1]
$ millions

	1983	1984	1985	1986	1987	1988	1989	1990	1991	1992
I. Agriculture and livestock	138	417	375	457	782	499	1 041	1 319	808	1 179
II. Mining and quarrying	3 864	3 908	4 186	2 440	3 400	3 204	3 387	4 795	3 945	3 919
Oil	3 665	3 637	3 612	2 008	2 956	2 777	2 950	4 324	3 410	3 497
Crude oil	3 242	3 373	3 321	1 808	2 711	2 434	2 456	3 519	2 456	2 632
Oil products	423	264	291	200	245	343	494	805	954	865
Other	199	271	574	432	444	427	437	471	535	422
III. Industrial products	5 177	6 432	7 052	8 302	10 101	10 580	11 325	16 189	16 294	17 773
Agriculture-based processed products	203	434	486	480	720	738	843	1 401	1 162	1 139
Industrial products	4 974	5 998	6 565	7 822	9 381	9 842	10 482	14 788	15 132	16 634
Chemicals	1 032	1 212	1 111	1 263	1 638	1 781	1 710	2 083	2 150	2 315
Fertiliser	119	128	183	159	299	203	395	369	314	310
Rubber and plastics	251	359	343	372	488	525	485	804	841	979
Textiles	98	117	146	161	204	260	297	579	557	730
Glass and ceramics	57	63	63	96	117	141	126	182	181	196
Iron and steel	675	862	1 060	1 028	1 537	1 655	2 217	1 931	2 011	2 118
Non-ferrous metals	195	220	224	230	418	412	421	537	451	425
Metal products	30	34	38	51	56	62	57	106	120	135
Machinery	1 432	1 618	1 551	2 304	2 454	2 400	2 188	3 754	3 756	4 042
Electrical appliances	398	573	664	892	940	1 075	1 028	1 570	1 858	1 746
Motor vehicles	478	517	812	768	550	690	795	1 603	1 558	2 239
Other industrial products	209	295	370	498	680	638	763	1 270	1 335	1 399
IV. Imports with waiver	56	–	–	–	–	–	–	–	–	–
Total	9 235	10 757	11 613	11 199	14 283	14 283	15 753	22 303	21 047	22 871

1. Excluding transit trade.
Source: State Institute of Statistics, *Monthly Indicators.*

Table F. Exports by commodities[1]
$ million

	1983	1984	1985	1986	1987	1988	1989	1990	1991	1992
I. Agricultural products	1 881	1 749	1 719	1 886	1 853	2 341	2 127	2 349	2 683	2 203
Cereals	376	267	234	246	266	441	315	342	522	616
Fruits and vegetables	591	646	561	820	800	867	789	1 068	1 045	932
Industrial crops and forestry products	531	492	659	495	431	696	693	667	848	465
Live animals and sea products	382	343	265	325	356	337	330	272	268	190
II. Mining and quarrying products	189	240	244	247	272	377	377	331	286	264
III. Processed and manufactured products	3 658	5 144	5 995	5 324	8 065	8 944	9 088	10 284	10 626	12 252
Processed agricultural products	670	808	647	667	954	885	919	940	1 212	1 337
Manufactured products	2 988	4 336	5 348	4 657	7 111	8 059	8 169	9 344	9 414	10 915
Textiles and clothing	1 299	1 875	1 790	1 851	2 707	3 201	3 509	4 061	4 328	5 268
Hides and leather	192	401	484	345	722	514	605	748	620	568
Forestry	15	24	106	52	32	22	16	21	16	28
Chemicals	120	173	266	350	527	734	774	616	464	491
Rubber and plastics	77	97	108	141	258	352	313	236	316	380
Petroleum products	232	409	372	178	232	331	254	287	277	231
Glass and ceramics	108	146	190	158	205	233	258	329	358	395
Cement	81	56	44	27	7	7	34	77	111	139
Iron and steel	407	576	969	804	852	1 458	1 349	1 613	1 452	1 558
Non-ferrous metals	79	86	116	111	134	226	266	262	174	164
Metal products and machinery	122	134	450	263	788	383	219	230	265	398
Electrical equipment and products	69	100	119	130	293	294	234	438	533	591
Other	187	259	334	247	354	304	340	426	500	700
Total	5 728	7 133	7 958	7 457	10 190	11 662	11 627	12 959	13 595	14 719

1. Excluding transit trade.
Source: State Institute of Statistics, *Monthly Indicators.*

122

Table G. Geographic distribution of foreign trade [1]

$ million

	Imports (cif)						Exports (fob)					
	1987	1988	1989	1990	1991	1992	1987	1988	1989	1990	1991	1992
OECD countries	9 031	9 237	9 908	14 225	14 071	15 438	6 444	6 707	7 184	8 810	8 856	9 348
EEC countries	5 668	5 894	6 059	9 332	9 221	10 050	4 867	5 098	5 416	6 893	7 042	7 603
of which:												
France	609	829	748	1 341	1 227	1 350	500	499	598	737	688	809
Germany	2 110	2 054	2 205	3 500	3 231	3 756	2 184	2 149	2 177	3 064	3 413	3 660
Italy	1 076	1 006	1 070	1 727	1 845	1 919	851	955	978	1 106	972	943
United Kingdom	697	739	728	1 014	1 166	1 187	541	576	616	745	676	797
Other OECD countries	3 363	3 343	3 849	4 893	4 850	5 388	1 577	1 609	1 768	1 917	1 814	1 745
of which:												
Japan	666	555	530	1 119	1 092	1 112	150	209	233	239	226	163
Switzerland	365	344	412	537	489	703	356	265	175	293	246	223
United States	1 363	1 520	2 088	2 283	2 241	2 601	713	761	970	968	913	865
Eastern European countries	969	1 102	1 493	2 256	2 066	2 211	334	609	1 029	987	1 262	694
Middle East and North Africa	3 152	2 935	2 927	3 939	3 188	3 415	3 084	3 530	2 876	2 498	2 729	2 784
of which:												
Iran	947	660	233	578	91	365	440	546	561	496	487	455
Iraq	1 154	1 441	1 650	1 047	0	1	945	986	446	214	122	212
Kuwait	75	89	81	54	0	68	248	199	168	92	16	66
Libya	305	79	286	487	281	446	141	218	227	220	237	108
Saudi Arabia	168	229	212	724	1 829	1 665	408	359	365	338	475	486
Other countries	1 131	1 100	1 435	1 886	1 729	1 807	328	816	539	665	750	1 892
Total	14 283	14 374	15 763	22 306	21 054	22 871	10 190	11 662	11 628	12 960	13 597	14 719

1. Excluding transit trade and non-monetary gold imports.
Source: State Institute of Statistics, *Monthly Indicators.*

123

Table H. **Balance of payments**[1]

$ million

	1984	1985	1986	1987	1988	1989	1990	1991	1992
Current account									
Exports, fob	7 389	8 255	7 583	10 322	11 929	11 780	13 026	13 667	14 891
Imports, fob	-10 331	-11 230	-10 664	-13 551	-13 706	-15 999	-22 581	-21 007	-23 082
Trade balance	-2 942	-2 975	-3 081	-3 229	-1 777	-4 219	-9 555	-7 340	-8 191
Services and income, credit	2 366	3 162	3 338	4 195	6 026	7 098	8 933	9 315	10 451
Tourism	548	1 094	950	1 476	2 355	2 557	3 225	2 654	3 639
Investment income	146	544	642	680	748	1 266	1 658	1 635	1 999
Other	1 672	1 524	1 746	2 039	2 923	3 275	4 050	5 026	4 813
Services and income, debit	-2 945	-3 184	-3 646	-4 162	-4 812	-5 476	-6 496	-6 816	-7 262
Tourism	-277	-324	-313	-448	-358	-565	-520	-592	-776
Investment income	-1 586	-1 753	-2 134	-2 387	-2 799	-2 907	-3 264	-3 430	-3 217
Other	-1 082	-1 107	-1 199	-1 327	-1 655	-2 004	-2 712	-2 794	-3 269
Private transfers, net	1 885	1 762	1 703	2 066	1 827	3 135	3 349	2 854	3 147
Workers' remittances	1 807	1 714	1 634	2 021	1 776	3 040	3 246	2 819	3 008
Other	78	48	69	45	51	95	103	35	139
Official transfers, net	197	222	221	324	332	423	1 144	2 245	912
Invisibles balance	1 503	1 962	1 616	2 423	3 373	5 180	6 930	7 598	7 248
Current balance	-1 439	-1 013	-1 465	-806	1 596	961	-2 625	258	-943
Capital account									
Direct investment	113	99	125	106	354	663	700	783	779
Portfolio investment	0	0	146	282	1 178	1 586	547	648	2 411
Credit utilisation	2 953	2 185	2 552	3 385	3 124	2 620	3 679	3 784	3 523
Debt repayments	-1 907	-2 208	-2 173	-2 687	-3 927	-4 023	-3 938	-4 095	-4 871
Dresdner Bank scheme, net	568	186	662	755	594	518	49	-497	410
Capital balance	1 727	262	1 312	1 841	1 323	1 364	1 037	623	2 252
Basic balance	288	-751	-153	1 035	2 919	2 325	-1 588	881	1 309
Short-term capital	-652	1 479	812	50	-2 281	-584	3 000	-3 020	1 395
Assets	-1 625	127	-313	-945	-1 428	371	-409	-2 563	-2 437
Liabilities	973	1 352	1 125	995	-853	-955	3 409	-457	3 832
Errors and omissions	469	-837	-118	-506	515	971	-468	940	-1 221
Counterpart items	-171	233	249	390	-263	50	364	170	0
Overall balance	-66	124	790	969	890	2 762	1 308	-1 029	1 484
Change in official reserves	66	-124	-790	-969	-890	-2 762	-1 308	1 029	-1 484
IMF	-138	-104	-245	-320	-469	-252	-1 255	1 029	-1 484
Official reserves	204	-20	-545	-649	-421	-2 510	-53	0	0

1. The Central Bank revised balance-of-payments statistics in 1989. In the new series, interest and debt repayments and credit utilisation figures include debt relief adjustments.
Source: Central Bank of Turkey, *Quarterly Bulletin.*

Table I.   External debt of Turkey [1]
Disbursed debt – End of period
$ million

	1984	1985	1986	1987	1988	1989	1990	1991	1992	1993 june
Medium- and long-term debt	17 479	20 717	25 752	32 605	34 305	36 006	39 536	41 372	42 932	44 896
Multilateral organisations	5 020	6 309	7 839	9 802	9 192	8 740	9 564	10 069	9 160	9 043
IMF	1 426	1 326	1 085	770	299	48	0	0	0	0
World Bank, IDA, IFC	2 590	3 661	4 917	6 550	6 421	6 137	6 435	6 540	5 761	5 695
European Investment Bank	394	453	571	675	583	561	604	602	463	313
European Resettlement Fund	554	815	1 216	1 757	1 836	1 918	2 439	2 859	2 880	2 999
Islamic Development Bank	12	12	12	15	22	51	68	54	40	22
OPEC Fund	40	35	30	25	20	15	10	5	3	2
International Fund for Agricultural Development	4	7	8	10	11	10	8	9	13	12
Bilateral credits	7 242	8 122	9 646	11 680	11 382	11 431	12 984	14 587	15 035	15 346
OECD countries	5 998	6 647	8 049	10 086	10 038	9 992	11 652	13 169	13 542	13 931
OPEC countries	761	915	1 013	1 066	886	697	564	438	363	340
Other countries	483	560	584	528	458	742	768	980	1 130	1 075
Commercial banks	3 541	4 159	4 969	6 391	8 891	10 269	10 721	10 992	12 956	14 506
Private lenders	1 676	2 127	3 298	4 732	4 840	5 566	6 267	5 724	5 781	6 001
Dresdner Bank scheme	1 326	1 858	3 069	4 569	4 723	5 500	6 255	5 713	5 771	5 992
Short-term debt	3 180	4 759	6 349	7 623	6 417	5 745	9 500	9 117	12 660	14 485
Commercial banks	1 006	1 495	2 673	3 725	2 950	1 841	3 845	4 144	6 490	7 327
Private lenders	2 174	3 264	3 676	3 898	3 467	3 904	5 655	4 973	6 170	7 158
Foreign exchange deposits	996	1 562	1 986	2 619	2 433	2 795	3 976	2 983	2 595	2 607
Total debt	20 659	25 476	32 101	40 228	40 722	41 751	49 036	50 489	55 592	59 381
Memorandum items (per cent)										
Total debt/GNP	41.0	47.5	54.7	59.0	57.5	52.0	44.5	46.5	49.1	
Medium- and long-term debt/GNP	34.7	38.6	43.8	47.8	48.4	44.8	36.9	38.1	37.9	
Short-term debt/GNP	6.3	8.9	10.9	11.2	9.1	7.2	8.6	8.4	11.2	
Short-term debt/total debt	15.4	18.7	19.8	18.9	15.8	13.7	19.4	18.1	22.8	
Total debt/exports of goods and services	177.2	193.2	255.8	243.5	207.6	186.3	185.3	184.0	189.1	
Total debt by borrower										
General government	53.3	50.4	51.3	52.3	56.8	57.3	52.2	54.3	51.2	
SEEs	6.9	8.3	9.2	9.2	9.8	9.9	12.6	10.2	9.2	
Central Bank	27.3	26.4	23.7	23.9	20.6	18.9	16.6	14.0	12.1	
Private sector	12.5	14.9	15.8	14.6	12.8	13.9	18.6	21.5	27.5	

1. In 1991, the Turkish authorities issued a new series of external debt statistics, starting from 1984. Revised series reflect the adjustment for valuation changes in World Bank loans arising from the World Bank's currency pool system and the reclassification of the Dresdner Bank accounts according to maturities. Foreign Military Sales (FMS) refinancing credits are also included. In 1988, $1 503 million and in 1989 $403 million FMS loans were rescheduled by a group of US bank under US Treasury guarantee. Other military debt is excluded.

Source: Data provided by the Under-Secretariat of the Treasury and the Foreign Trade, and Central Bank of Turkey.

Table J. **Public sector borrowing**

	1983	1984	1985	1986	1987	1988	1989	1990	1991	1992
Public sector deficit (TL billion)	-687	-1 194	-1 267	-1 869	-4 563	-6 235	-12 283	-29 324	-65 617	-116 492
General government	-385	-773	-397	-549	-2 093	-3 430	-7 863	-14 338	-45 674	-80 179
State economic enterprises (SEEs)	-302	-421	-870	-1 320	-2 470	-2 805	-4 420	-14 986	-19 943	-36 313
Public sector deficit/GNP	-6.0	-6.5	-4.6	-4.7	-7.8	-6.3	-7.2	-10.2	-14.5	-14.9
General government	-3.3	-4.2	-1.5	-1.3	-3.6	-3.5	-4.6	-4.9	-10.1	-10.2
Central government	-2.7	-5.3	-2.9	-3.6	-4.5	-4.0	-4.5	-4.2	-7.4	-6.1
Local administrations	0.0	0.1	0.1	-0.3	-0.6	-0.5	-0.3	0.0	-0.6	-1.1
Revolving funds	-0.6	0.0	0.5	0.4	0.8	0.3	0.5	0.4	-0.2	-0.3
Extra-budgetary funds[1]	–	1.0	0.8	2.2	0.7	0.7	-0.3	-1.2	-1.8	-2.8
SEEs[2]	-2.7	-2.3	-3.1	-3.4	-4.2	-2.8	-2.6	-5.3	-4.4	-4.7
Sources of financing (per cent of total)										
Central Bank	10.5	11.2	27.3	14.1	20.4	15.8	3.7	1.5	16.5	20.1
Foreign borrowing, net	16.6	54.1	1.7	58.0	44.2	43.3	15.5	12.7	3.3	14
Domestic borrowing, net[3]	72.9	34.5	71.0	27.9	35.4	40.9	80.8	85.8	80.2	65.9
Memorandum items:										
Public debt/GNP										
General government	43.8	47.3	49.9	55.5	61.9	61.6	53.7	43.5	43.7	48.7
Domestic	27.5	25.3	25.6	27.0	31.0	29.7	25.3	20.2	20.0	23.4
Foreign	16.3	22.0	24.3	28.5	30.9	31.9	28.4	23.3	23.7	25.3
SEEs										
Domestic	n.a.	n.a.	n.a.	n.a.	n.a.	n.a.	n.a.	n.a.	n.a.	n.a.
Foreign	3.1	3.0	3.9	5.6	6.4	5.6	5.1	4.4	4.5	4.5

1. Including State economic enterprises in the process of privatisation.
2. Including non-financial SEE's.
3. Including short-term borrowing.
Source: Data provided by the State Planning Organisation, and OECD estimates.

126

Table K. **Money and banking**

TL billion, end of period

	1986	1987	1988	1989	1990	1991	1992
Money supply							
Notes and coins	1 302	2 212	3 426	6 840	11 378	17 449	30 389
Sight deposits	3 953	6 417	7 886	12 718	20 020	29 344	47 952
M1	5 255	8 629	11 312	19 558	31 398	46 793	78 341
Time deposits	6 918	9 019	15 883	27 582	40 172	70 325	112 395
M2	12 173	17 648	27 194	47 139	71 570	117 118	190 736
Foreign exchange deposits	2 436	5 356	9 512	14 135	21 793	50 936	103 234
M2X	14 609	23 004	36 707	61 274	93 363	168 054	293 970
Central Bank							
Total assets	14 020	22 322	38 362	48 988	60 987	96 789	177 244
Foreign assets	3 301	4 778	11 429	17 948	25 583	38 736	75 758
Domestic assets	10 719	17 544	26 933	31 040	35 404	58 053	101 486
Cash credits	4 624	7 524	10 039	10 892	10 644	28 199	72 044
Credit to public sector	3 887	5 607	7 020	7 860	5 324	22 904	62 602
Credit to private sector	737	1 917	3 019	3 032	5 320	5 295	9 442
Other items	146	212	–287	–1 058	–1 648	–2 575	–5 293
Devaluation account	5 949	9 809	17 181	21 206	26 408	32 429	34 735
Total liabilities	14 020	22 322	38 362	48 988	60 987	96 789	177 244
Reserve money	3 999	5 503	10 143	17 035	23 871	37 244	61 195
Monetary base	4 037	5 993	11 349	17 365	22 944	42 828	82 974
Central bank money	4 297	6 430	11 852	18 528	23 837	43 993	87 837
Foreign currency liabilities	9 724	15 892	26 511	30 460	37 150	52 796	89 407
Deposit money banks							
Deposits[1]	15 595	23 898	38 013	61 648	93 931	164 669	296 151
Credits	10 219	16 439	23 871	39 357	69 287	106 491	195 182
Total bank credits							
(net of Central Bank advances to banks)	13 031	20 133	29 012	43 580	74 659	130 796	244 420
Central bank	1 942	2 644	3 509	3 506	4 449	18 454	42 584
Deposit money banks	10 042	16 024	22 769	36 522	65 198	101 452	185 419
Investment banks	1 047	1 465	2 734	3 552	5 012	10 890	16 418

1. Including interbank and foreign currency deposits.
Source: Central Bank of Turkey, Quarterly Bulletin.

Table L. Central government budget

TL billion

	1983	1984	1985	1986	1987	1988	1989	1990	1991	1992
Revenues	2 300	2 805	4 526	6 758	10 089	17 016	30 379	55 239	96 747	174 224
Tax revenues	1 935	2 372	3 829	5 972	9 051	14 232	25 550	45 400	78 638	141 602
Non-tax revenues	366	433	697	786	1 038	2 784	4 829	9 839	18 109	32 622
Expenditures	2 613	3 784	5 313	8 165	12 696	21 006	38 051	67 194	130 263	221 658
Current personnel expenditures	670	896	1 275	1 840	2 996	5 053	12 539	26 465	49 291	94 076
Other current expenditures	398	594	820	1 211	1 542	2 391	4 068	6 916	11 112	20 145
Investment	473	691	1 030	1 624	2 296	3 141	5 067	8 902	17 146	29 239
Transfers	1 071	1 603	2 188	3 490	5 864	10 421	16 378	24 911	52 714	78 198
of which: SEEs	302	275	181	138	445	1 014	1 214	1 252	12 191	8 145
Interest payment	211	441	675	1 331	2 266	4 978	8 260	13 966	24 073	40 298
Budget balance	–313	–979	–787	–1 407	–2 607	–3 990	–7 673	–11 955	–33 516	–47 434
Deferred payments	159	73	62	227	910	36	38	1 161	3 556	–778
Advance payments	–28	–120	–178	–424	–878	–117	–677	–1 561	–3 465	–11 227
Cash balance	–182	–1 026	–903	–1 604	–2 575	–4 071	–8 312	–12 355	–33 425	–59 439
Borrowing	259	764	863	2 027	2 976	6 478	12 571	18 012	22 399	55 375
Domestic	199	195	670	1 269	2 045	3 816	8 983	12 523	11 510	35 657
Foreign	60	569	193	758	931	2 662	3 588	5 489	10 889	19 718
Repayments	–180	–294	–592	–1 557	–2 346	–3 738	–6 798	–10 029	–18 199	–35 929
Domestic	–30	–58	–172	–793	–1 150	–1 383	–3 001	–4 581	–9 231	–20 249
Foreign	–150	–236	–420	–764	–1 197	–2 355	–3 797	–5 448	–8 968	–15 680
Short-term borrowing (net)	–24	473	498	925	1 268	1 064	1 452	2 263	23 508	41 372
Central Bank	72	190	266	257	355	675	457	331	10 719	17 394
Treasury bills	–96	284	232	668	913	389	995	1 932	12 789	23 978
Other borrowing[1]	127	82	135	209	677	266	1 086	2 109	5 718	–1 380

1. Including errors and omissions and change in cash/bank.
Source: Data submitted by the State Planning Organisation.

Table M. Central government budget revenues

New classification,[1] TL billion

	1985	1986	1987	1988	1989	1990	1991	1992
Taxes on income	1 772	3 053	4 425	6 919	13 469	23 246	40 418	70 134
Personal income tax	1 324	2 104	3 093	4 801	9 871	18 609	33 355	60 056
Corporate income tax	448	949	1 332	2 118	3 598	4 637	7 063	10 078
Taxes on wealth	54	53	68	147	176	411	676	1 259
Real estate tax[2]	30	..	..	..	..	..	..	..
Motor vehicles tax	17	43	51	121	134	329	539	1 020
Inheritance and gift tax	7	10	17	26	43	82	137	239
Taxes on goods and services	1 098	1 853	2 768	4 487	7 642	13 669	24 673	47 341
Domestic value-added tax (VAT)	567	1 040	1 563	2 661	4 177	7 650	14 541	27 053
Supplememtary VAT (monopoly products)	124	178	264	288	463	373	605	187
Petroleum consumption tax	46	54	71	159	656	1 224	2 370	6 769
Motor vehicles purchase tax	21	43	74	127	214	585	981	2 378
Banking and insurance tax	58	94	155	374	643	1 164	2 119	3 922
Stamp duty	181	250	379	534	876	1 497	2 457	4 153
Fees	101	194	262	344	613	1 176	1 600	2 879
Taxes on foreign trade	746	993	1 777	2 672	4 245	8 058	12 864	22 848
Customs duty	217	286	425	589	710	1 055	1 032	1 715
Customs duty on petroleum	6	6	6	11	14	8	4	10
VAT on imports	384	528	1 004	1 517	2 285	4 722	8 291	15 034
Stamp duty imports	74	117	259	439	968	1 554	2 526	4 438
Wharf duty	62	54	81	114	252	685	945	1 546
Other	3	2	2	2	16	34	66	105
Abolished taxes	159	20	13	7	18	16	7	20
Total tax revenues	3 829	5 972	9 051	14 232	25 550	45 400	78 638	141 602
Non-tax regular revenues	359	502	809	1 353	2 439	4 267	3 926	7 649
Corporate profits and State shares	28	33	45	63	111	206	318	536
Revenues of State property[3]	31	69	110	245	454	1 828	869	1 367
Interests and claims	37	59	88	109	348	246	267	404
Fines	75	111	165	328	522	698	853	2 533
Other revenues	188	230	401	608	1 004	1 289	1 619	2 809
Special revenues[4]	125	83	19	1 187	1 835	3 274	4 796	21 893
Grants	99	73	15	41	115	1 635	8 434	1 700
Total non-tax revenues	583	658	843	2 581	4 389	9 176	17 156	31 242
Annex budget revenues	114	128	195	203	440	663	953	1 380
Total consolidated budget revenues	4 526	6 758	10 089	17 016	30 379	55 239	96 747	174 224

1. With the introduction of value-added tax (VAT) in January 1985, the following taxes were abolished: Sales, communications and advertisement tax, production tax, production tax on petroleum and monopoly products.
2. From 1986 onwards real estate tax is collected by municipalities.
3. From 1990 onwards, privatisations revenues are included.
4. From 1992 onwards, transfers from Extra-budgetary Funds are included.
Source: Ministry of Finance and Customs.

Table N. Dollar exchange rate of the Turkish lira

TL per $

7th September 1946		2.80		**1984**		**364.63**
23rd August 1960		9.00			Q 1	307.68
10th August 1970		14.85			Q 2	346.15
28th December 1971		14.00			Q 3	385.19
16th February 1973		13.85			Q 4	419.51
15th August 1973		14.00		**1985**		**519.32**
14th May 1974		13.50			Q 1	468.33
20th September 1974		13.85			Q 2	516.52
17th April 1975		14.00			Q 3	535.91
8th July 1975		14.25			Q 4	556.53
8th August 1975		14.50		**1986**		**669.01**
28th August 1975		14.75			Q 1	598.93
28th October 1975		15.00			Q 2	666.38
15th March 1976		15.50			Q 3	676.76
4th April 1976		16.00			Q 4	733.96
27th October 1976		16.50		**1987**		**855.05**
1st March 1977		17.50			Q 1	761.15
21st September 1977		19.25			Q 2	808.67
1st March 1978		25.00			Q 3	886.82
10th April 1979		26.50	(47.10)[1]		Q 4	963.55
10th May 1979		26.50	(42.10)[1]	**1988**		**1 419.62**
10th June 1979		47.10[2]			Q 1	1 140.85
25th January 1980		70.00	(55.00)[3]		Q 2	1 294.41
2nd April 1980		73.70	(57.90)[3]		Q 3	1 498.87
9th June 1980		78.00	(61.30)[3]		Q 4	1 744.35
4th August 1980		80.00	(62.87)[3]	**1989**		**2 119.51**
11th October 1980		82.70	(65.19)[3]		Q 1	1 911.80
26th October 1980		84.80	(72.50)[3]		Q 2	2 079.15
9th November 1980		87.95	(77.50)[3]		Q 3	2 187.96
10th December 1980		89.25	(78.66)[3]		Q 4	2 299.11
27th January 1981		91.90	(79.41)[3]	**1990**		**2 606.29**
5th February 1981		95.95	(83.38)[3]		Q 1	2 386.28
24th March 1981		95.65	(83.12)[3]		Q 2	2 558.86
15th April 1981		98.20			Q 3	2 685.18
May 1981		101.92[4]			Q 4	2 794.83
1981		**110.13**		**1991**		**4 164.17**
	Q 1	93.58			Q 1	3 218.17
	Q 2	102.09			Q 2	3 984.37
	Q 3	117.70			Q 3	4 507.93
	Q 4	127.15			Q 4	4 946.21
1982		**160.82**		**1992**		**6 865.01**
	Q 1	140.83			Q 1	5 686.67
	Q 2	151.48			Q 2	6 667.32
	Q 3	169.91			Q 3	7 098.55
	Q 4	181.04			Q 4	8 007.50
1983		**223.82**		**1993**		**10 973.56**
	Q 1	192.53			Q 1	9 045.88
	Q 2	210.84			Q 2	9 990.17
	Q 3	232.95			Q 3	11 551.61
	Q 4	258.96			Q 4	13 306.57

1. Premium rate for workers' remittances and tourism revenues.
2. For exports of traditional agricultural goods and imports of petroleum and its products and fertiliser raw materials $ parity is kept at TL 35.00.
3. For imports of fertiliser and agricultural pesticides.
4. Since 1st May 1981, the exchange rate has been adjusted on a daily basis. The figures shown are averages of the daily exchange rates.
Source: Central Bank of Turkey, *Quarterly Bulletin.*

BASIC STATISTICS

BASIC STATISTICS:

INTERNATIONAL COMPARISONS

	Units	Reference period[1]	Australia	Austria	Belgium	Canada
Population						
Total	Thousands	1990	17 085	7 718	9 967	26 620
Inhabitants per sq. km	Number	1990	2	92	327	3
Net average annual increase over previous 10 years	%	1990	1.5	0.2	0.1	1
Employment						
Total civilian employment (TCE)[2]	Thousands	1990	7 850	3 412	3 726	12 572
Of which : Agriculture	% of TCE		5.6	7.9	2.7	4.2
Industry	% of TCE		25.4	36.8	28.3	24.6
Services	% of TCE		69	55.3	69	71.2
Gross domestic product (GDP)						
At current prices and current exchange rates	Bill US $	1990	294.1	157.4	192.4	570.1
Per capita	US $		17 215	20 391	19 303	21 418
At current prices using current PPP's[3]	Bill US $	1990	271.7	127.4	163	510.5
Per capita	US $		15 900	16 513	16 351	19 179
Average annual volume growth over previous 5 years	%	1990	3.1	3.1	3.2	3
Gross fixed capital formation (GFCF)	% of GDP	1990	22.9	24.3	20.3	21.4
Of which: Machinery and equipment	% of GDP		9.7	10.1	10.4	7.2
Residential construction	% of GDP	1990	4.8	4.6	4.3	6.8
Average annual volume growth over previous 5 years	%	1990	2.4	4.6	9.5	5.8
Gross saving ratio[4]	% of GDP	1990	19.7	26	21.8	17.4
General government						
Current expenditure on goods and services	% of GDP	1990	17.3	18	14.3	19.8
Current disbursements[5]	% of GDP	1990	34.9	44.9	53.1	44
Current receipts	% of GDP	1990	35.1	46.7	49.5	41.6
Net official development assistance	Mill US $	1990	0.34	0.25	0.45	0.44
Indicators of living standards						
Private consumption per capita using current PPP's[3]	US $	1990	9 441	9 154	10 119	11 323
Passenger cars per 1 000 inhabitants	Number	1989	570	416	416	613
Telephones per 1 000 inhabitants	Number	1989	550 (85)	540	500 (88)	780 (88
Television sets per 1 000 inhabitants	Number	1988	217	484 (89)	255	586
Doctors per 1 000 inhabitants	Number	1990	2.3	2.1	3.4	2.2
Infant mortality per 1 000 live births	Number	1990	8.2	7.8	7.9	7.2 (89
Wages and prices (average annual increase over previous 5 years)						
Wages (earnings or rates according to availability)	%	1990	5.6	5	3	4.3
Consumer prices	%	1990	7.9	2.2	2.1	4.5
Foreign trade						
Exports of goods, fob*	Mill US $	1990	39 813	40 985	118 291[7]	127 334
As % of GDP	%		13.5	26	61.5	22.3
Average annual increase over previous 5 years	%		11.9	19.1	17.1	7.8
Imports of goods, cif*	Mill US $	1990	38 907	48 914	120 330[7]	116 561
As % of GDP	%		13.2	31.1	62.5	20.4
Average annual increase over previous 5 years	%		11	18.6	16.5	8.8
Total official reserves[6]	Mill SDR's	1990	11 432	6 591	8 541[7]	12 544
As ratio of average monthly imports of goods	ratio		3.5	1.6	0.9	1.3

* At current prices and exchange rates.
1. Unless otherwise stated.
2. According to the definitions used in OECD Labour Force Statistics.
3. PPP's = Purchasing Power Parities.
4. Gross saving = Gross national disposable income minus Private and Government consumption.
5. Current disbursements = Current expenditure on goods and services plus current transfers and payments of property income.
6. Gold included in reserves is valued at 35 SDR's per ounce. End of year.
7. Including Luxembourg.
8. Included in Belgium.

EMPLOYMENT OPPORTUNITIES

Economics Department, OECD

The Economics Department of the OECD offers challenging and rewarding opportunities to economists interested in applied policy analysis in an international environment. The Department's concerns extend across the entire field of economic policy analysis, both macro-economic and micro-economic. Its main task is to provide, for discussion by committees of senior officials from Member countries, documents and papers dealing with current policy concerns. Within this programme of work, three major responsibilities are:

- to prepare regular surveys of the economies of individual Member countries;
- to issue full twice-yearly reviews of the economic situation and prospects of the OECD countries in the context of world economic trends;
- to analyse specific policy issues in a medium-term context for theOECD as a whole, and to a lesser extent for the non-OECD countries.

The documents prepared for these purposes, together with much of the Department's other economic work, appear in published form in the *OECD Economic Outlook, OECD Economic Surveys, OECD Economic Studies* and the Department's *Working Papers* series.

The Department maintains a world econometric model, INTERLINK, which plays an important role in the preparation of the policy analyses and twice-yearly projections. The availability of extensive cross-country data bases and good computer resources facilitates comparative empirical analysis, much of which is incorporated into the model.

The Department is made up of about 75 professional economists from a variety of backgrounds and Member countries. Most projects are carried out by small teams and last from four to eighteen months. Within the Department, ideas and points of view are widely discussed; there is a lively professional interchange, and all professional staff have the opportunity to contribute actively to the programme of work.

Skills the Economics Department is looking for:

a) Solid competence in using the tools of both micro-economic and macro-economic theory to answer policy questions. Experience indicates that this normally requires the equivalent of a PH.D. in economics or substantial relevant professional experience to compensate for a lower degree.

b) Solid knowledge of economic statistics and quantitative methods; this includes how to identify data, estimate structural relationships, apply basic techniques of time series analysis, and test hypotheses. It is essential to be able to interpret results sensibly in an economic policy context.

c) A keen interest in and knowledge of policy issues, economic developments and their political/social contexts.

d) Interest and experience in analysing questions posed by policy-makers and presenting the results to them effectively and judiciously. Thus, work experience in government agencies or policy research institutions is an advantage.

e) The ability to write clearly, effectively, and to the point. The OECD is a bilingual organisation with French and English as the official languages. Candidates must have excellent knowledge of one of these languages, and some knowledge of the other. Knowledge of other languages might also be an advantage for certain posts.

f) For some posts, expertise in a particular area may be important, but a successful candidate is expected to be able to work on a broader range of topics relevant to the work of the Department. Thus, except in rare cases, the Department does not recruit narrow specialists.

g) The Department works on a tight time schedule and strict deadlines. Moreover, much of the work in the Department is carried out in small groups of economists. Thus, the ability to work with other economists from a variety of cultural and professional backgrounds, to supervise junior staff, and to produce work on time is important.

General Information

The salary for recruits depends on educational and professional background. Positions carry a basic salary from FF 262 512 or FF 323 916 for Administrators (economists) and from FF 375 708 for Principal Administrators (senior economists). This may be supplemented by expatriation and/or family allowances, depending on nationality, residence and family situation. Initial appointments are for a fixed term of two to three years.

Vacancies are open to candidates from OECD Member countries. The Organisation seeks to maintain an appropriate balance between female and male staff and among nationals from Member countries.

For further information on employment opportunities in the Economics Department, contact:

Administrative Unit
Economics Department
OECD
2, rue André-Pascal
75775 PARIS CEDEX 16
FRANCE

Applications citing ''ECSUR'', together with a detailed *curriculum vitae* in English or French, should be sent to the Head of Personnel at the above address.

MAIN SALES OUTLETS OF OECD PUBLICATIONS
PRINCIPAUX POINTS DE VENTE DES PUBLICATIONS DE L'OCDE

ARGENTINA – ARGENTINE
Carlos Hirsch S.R.L.
Galería Güemes, Florida 165, 4° Piso
1333 Buenos Aires   Tel. (1) 331.1787 y 331.2391
Telefax: (1) 331.1787

AUSTRALIA – AUSTRALIE
D.A. Information Services
648 Whitehorse Road, P.O.B 163
Mitcham, Victoria 3132   Tel. (03) 873.4411
Telefax: (03) 873.5679

AUSTRIA – AUTRICHE
Gerold & Co.
Graben 31
Wien I   Tel. (0222) 533.50.14

BELGIUM – BELGIQUE
Jean De Lannoy
Avenue du Roi 202
B-1060 Bruxelles   Tel. (02) 538.51.69/538.08.41
Telefax: (02) 538.08.41

CANADA
Renouf Publishing Company Ltd.
1294 Algoma Road
Ottawa, ON K1B 3W8   Tel. (613) 741.4333
Telefax: (613) 741.5439
Stores:
61 Sparks Street
Ottawa, ON K1P 5R1   Tel. (613) 238.8985
211 Yonge Street
Toronto, ON M5B 1M4   Tel. (416) 363.3171
Telefax: (416)363.59.63

Les Éditions La Liberté Inc.
3020 Chemin Sainte-Foy
Sainte-Foy, PQ G1X 3V6   Tel. (418) 658.3763
Telefax: (418) 658.3763

Federal Publications Inc.
165 University Avenue, Suite 701
Toronto, ON M5H 3B8   Tel. (416) 860.1611
Telefax: (416) 860.1608

Les Publications Fédérales
1185 Université
Montréal, QC H3B 3A7   Tel. (514) 954.1633
Telefax : (514) 954.1635

CHINA – CHINE
China National Publications Import
Export Corporation (CNPIEC)
16 Gongti E. Road, Chaoyang District
P.O. Box 88 or 50
Beijing 100704 PR   Tel. (01) 506.6688
Telefax: (01) 506.3101

DENMARK – DANEMARK
Munksgaard Book and Subscription Service
35, Nørre Søgade, P.O. Box 2148
DK-1016 København K   Tel. (33) 12.85.70
Telefax: (33) 12.93.87

FINLAND – FINLANDE
Akateeminen Kirjakauppa
Keskuskatu 1, P.O. Box 128
00100 Helsinki
Subscription Services/Agence d'abonnements :
P.O. Box 23
00371 Helsinki   Tel. (358 0) 12141
Telefax: (358 0) 121.4450

FRANCE
OECD/OCDE
Mail Orders/Commandes par correspondance:
2, rue André-Pascal
75775 Paris Cedex 16   Tel. (33-1) 45.24.82.00
Telefax: (33-1) 49.10.42.76
Telex: 640048 OCDE

OECD Bookshop/Librairie de l'OCDE :
33, rue Octave-Feuillet
75016 Paris   Tel. (33-1) 45.24.81.67
(33-1) 45.24.81.81
Documentation Française
29, quai Voltaire
75007 Paris   Tel. 40.15.70.00
Gibert Jeune (Droit-Économie)
6, place Saint-Michel
75006 Paris   Tel. 43.25.91.19
Librairie du Commerce International
10, avenue d'Iéna
75016 Paris   Tel. 40.73.34.60
Librairie Dunod
Université Paris-Dauphine
Place du Maréchal de Lattre de Tassigny
75016 Paris   Tel. (1) 44.05.40.13
Librairie Lavoisier
11, rue Lavoisier
75008 Paris   Tel. 42.65.39.95
Librairie L.G.D.J. - Montchrestien
20, rue Soufflot
75005 Paris   Tel. 46.33.89.85
Librairie des Sciences Politiques
30, rue Saint-Guillaume
75007 Paris   Tel. 45.48.36.02
P.U.F.
49, boulevard Saint-Michel
75005 Paris   Tel. 43.25.83.40
Librairie de l'Université
12a, rue Nazareth
13100 Aix-en-Provence   Tel. (16) 42.26.18.08
Documentation Française
165, rue Garibaldi
69003 Lyon   Tel. (16) 78.63.32.23
Librairie Decitre
29, place Bellecour
69002 Lyon   Tel. (16) 72.40.54.54

GERMANY – ALLEMAGNE
OECD Publications and Information Centre
August-Bebel-Allee 6
D-53175 Bonn 2   Tel. (0228) 959.120
Telefax: (0228) 959.12.17

GREECE – GRÈCE
Librairie Kauffmann
Mavrokordatou 9
106 78 Athens   Tel. (01) 32.55.321
Telefax: (01) 36.33.967

HONG-KONG
Swindon Book Co. Ltd.
13–15 Lock Road
Kowloon, Hong Kong   Tel. 366.80.31
Telefax: 739.49.75

HUNGARY – HONGRIE
Euro Info Service
POB 1271
1464 Budapest   Tel. (1) 111.62.16
Telefax : (1) 111.60.61

ICELAND – ISLANDE
Mál Mog Menning
Laugavegi 18, Pósthólf 392
121 Reykjavik   Tel. 162.35.23

INDIA – INDE
Oxford Book and Stationery Co.
Scindia House
New Delhi 110001   Tel.(11) 331.5896/5308
Telefax: (11) 332.5993
17 Park Street
Calcutta 700016   Tel. 240832

INDONESIA – INDONÉSIE
Pdii-Lipi
P.O. Box 269/JKSMG/88
Jakarta 12790   Tel. 583467
Telex: 62 875

IRELAND – IRLANDE
TDC Publishers – Library Suppliers
12 North Frederick Street
Dublin 1   Tel. (01) 874.48.35
Telefax: (01) 874.84.16

ISRAEL
Electronic Publications only
Publications électroniques seulement
Praedicta
5 Shatna Street
P.O. Box 34030
Jerusalem 91340   Tel. (2) 52.84.90/1/2
Telefax: (2) 52.84.93

ITALY – ITALIE
Libreria Commissionaria Sansoni
Via Duca di Calabria 1/1
50125 Firenze   Tel. (055) 64.54.15
Telefax: (055) 64.12.57
Via Bartolini 29
20155 Milano   Tel. (02) 36.50.83
Editrice e Libreria Herder
Piazza Montecitorio 120
00186 Roma   Tel. 679.46.28
Telefax: 678.47.51
Libreria Hoepli
Via Hoepli 5
20121 Milano   Tel. (02) 86.54.46
Telefax: (02) 805.28.86
Libreria Scientifica
Dott. Lucio de Biasio 'Aeiou'
Via Coronelli, 6
20146 Milano   Tel. (02) 48.95.45.52
Telefax: (02) 48.95.45.48

JAPAN – JAPON
OECD Publications and Information Centre
Landic Akasaka Building
2-3-4 Akasaka, Minato-ku
Tokyo 107   Tel. (81.3) 3586.2016
Telefax: (81.3) 3584.7929

KOREA – CORÉE
Kyobo Book Centre Co. Ltd.
P.O. Box 1658, Kwang Hwa Moon
Seoul   Tel. 730.78.91
Telefax: 735.00.30

MALAYSIA – MALAISIE
Co-operative Bookshop Ltd.
University of Malaya
P.O. Box 1127, Jalan Pantai Baru
59700 Kuala Lumpur
Malaysia   Tel. 756.5000/756.5425
Telefax: 757.3661

MEXICO – MEXIQUE
Revistas y Periodicos Internacionales S.A. de C.V.
Florencia 57 - 1004
Mexico, D.F. 06600   Tel. 207.81.00
Telefax : 208.39.79

NETHERLANDS – PAYS-BAS
SDU Uitgeverij Plantijnstraat
Externe Fondsen
Postbus 20014
2500 EA's-Gravenhage   Tel. (070) 37.89.880
Voor bestellingen: Telefax: (070) 34.75.778

PRINTED IN FRANCE

•

OECD PUBLICATIONS
2 rue André-Pascal
75775 PARIS CEDEX 16
No. 47143
(10 94 27 1) ISBN 92-64-14099-9
ISSN 0376-6438

•